CONTENTS

1

THE EARLY HISTORY
OF HURLING

AN ANCIENT GAME

Legend has it that the first recorded reference to hurling dates from a battle fought at Moytura, near Cong, County Mayo in 1272 BC between the native Fir Bolg and the invading Tuatha dé Danann, who were demanding half the country. When their demand was refused a battle was inevitable. While the sides were preparing for the fray it was agreed to have a hurling contest between twenty-seven of the best players from each side.

The match began. Many a blow was dealt on legs and arms 'till their bones were bruised and broken and they fell outstretched on the turf and the match ended.' The Fir Bolg won and then fell upon their opponents and slew them. However, even though they won the battle they lost the war because the Tuatha dé Danann eventually won the right to settle in Ireland.

ORIGIN OF HURLING

The fact that each side knew how to play the game before the battle suggests that hurling was already well established in Ireland in 1272 BC. Where the game originated, nobody can tell. It is probably true that since time immemorial people have been striking a ball with a stick for recreation. There is a carved panel in the National Museum of Greece dating from the fifth century BC that shows two figures facing each other in a crouched position, holding two crooked sticks with a ball between them as if waiting for the signal to begin the game. This might suggest a similar game was played in Greece. As far as can be ascertained there is no other comparable game to it anywhere in Europe. It would appear that hurling was well established when the Celts arrived in Ireland and must have originated with some earlier group of settlers.

THE TAILTEANN GAMES

According to legend, one of the kings of the Tuatha dé Danann, named Lú, who lived before the tenth century BC, was a patron of public sports and started the annual Aonach Tailteann or Tailteann Fair. The first fair is reputed to have been held in the 'year of the world 3370'. The fair used to be held on 1 August. The Fair of Tailteann appears to have been in the nature of an Olympic Games and was where the men of Ireland came together to indulge in such sports as chariot racing, horse racing and hurling. The fair was held continuously down to the time of the last King of Ireland, Ruairí Ó Conchúir, in the twelfth century. The name was revived in 1924 when the Free State Government held a great Celtic cultural festival, which included hurling teams from among the Irish Diaspora, and held it again in 1928 and 1932.

HURLING IN MYTH AND LEGEND

In the centuries before and after the beginning of the Christian era there are many references to hurling in the myths and legends of Ireland. Six centuries before Christ, the King of Leinster's son, Maon, who was born dumb, is said to have recovered his speech in a most unusual way. In spite of all the attentions of the wisest men of the day, he entered adult life as a mute and was forced to accept the regency of his uncle. However, he had one consolation in that he played hurling. One day, during a game, he received such a severe blow to his shin from an opponent's hurley that it brought a yelp of pain out of him. His companions were amazed and, like Archimedes after his epiphany in the bathtub, began to shout 'Labhraidh Maon, Labhraidh Maon' (Maon spoke). The name Maon, meaning dumb, was quickly forgotten and in its place Labhraidh, the speaker, King of Leinster, entered his inheritance.

HOW SETANTA BECAME CUCHULAINN

Setanta was a noble youth and the greatest hurler in ancient times. He lived with his uncle, Conchúr, the King of Ulster. One day Conchúr was invited to the house of his blacksmith, Culann. He decided to bring Setanta with him. At the time of departure Setanta was in the middle of an important game of hurling and promised to follow his uncle as soon as the game was finished. Just before the meal started in the house of Culann, the host asked if all the guests had arrived and Conchúr, forgetting about Setanta, said they had. So Culann released a savage hound to guard the house during the feast.

When Setanta finished his game he set out for Culann's home, hurling the ball and throwing his spear along the journey. When he arrived at the home, the hound sprang at him with gnashing teeth. He had the ball in his hand and, to protect himself, he flung it with all his might down the hound's throat. The animal was halted in his tracks, choked and collapsed to the ground, howling as it expired.

On hearing the commotion all those inside the house fell silent. Conchúr suddenly remembered Setanta and a look of horror crossed his face. All the guests believed Setanta to be killed. The servants were despatched to find out but were amazed to find Setanta standing over the dead hound. The king was overjoyed to find his nephew alive. However, when Culann heard of the death of his hound he was angry and complained of the loss of the best watchdog in the land. Setanta promised to find another dog for his host. In the meantime he promised that he himself would guard the house of Culann and become his watchdog. And with that Conchúr said that in future he would be known as Cú Chulainn, the hound of Culann.

DECLARATION OF LOVE TO A HURLER

One of the great love stories in Irish myth and legend is that of Diarmuid and Grainne. Grainne was betrothed to the aging Fionn MacCumhaill, when she spotted Diarmuid on the hurling field and fell in love with him. She describes what happened in this speech:

> Of a day when a hurling match was played on the green of Tara, between Mac Lú and the Fiann on the one side and Caibre of the Liffey and the men of Tara on the other, I sat high up at the window of my sunny chamber to see the game. Thou didst remain sitting with some other that day, not meaning to take part in the play. But, at last, when the game began to go against thy friends, I saw thee start up and, snatching the hurley from the man nearest to thee, thou didst rush into the thick of the crowd and before sitting down thou didst win the goal three times on the men of Tara. At that hour my eyes and my heart were turned to thee and well I knew thee today in this banquet hall, though not thy name till the druid told me. At that same hour too I gave thee my love, what I never gave, and never will give, to any other.

She persuaded Diarmuid to run away with her. They were pursued by Fionn and the Fianna and, after an epic chase, Diarmuid was killed by a boar, bringing great sadness to Grainne.

LAWS AGAINST HURLING

The Anglo-Normans came to Ireland in the second half of the twelfth century and gradually established sway over most of the country. They were supposed to be a 'civilising' force but instead succumbed to Irish ways and took such an interest in hurling that the authorities came to regard it as a threat to the security of the colony. A law was passed in 1366 to wean the Normans from a game from which 'great evils and maims have arisen.' The country was in a sorry mess as the preamble to the legislation stated:

By now many English of the said land, forsaking the English language, fashion, mode of riding, laws and usages, live and govern themselves according to the manners, fashion and language of the Irish enemies, and also have made divers marriages and alliances between themselves and the Irish enemies aforesaid, whereby the said land and the liege people thereof, the English language, the allegiance due to our Lord the King, and the English laws there are put in subjection and decayed and the Irish enemies exalted and raised up contrary to right.'

One of the best-known parts of the legislation singled out hurling for special mention:

… it is ordained and established that the commons of the said land of Ireland … use not henceforth the games which men call hurlings with great clubs of a ball on the ground from which great evils and mains have arisen, to the weakening of the defence of the said land …

STATUTE OF GALWAY

The above law, known as the Statute of Kilkenny, didn't have the desired effect, for hurling had to be outlawed again by the Galway Statute of 1537. The following article from the statute is so urgent and precise that it suggests a certain irritation on the part of the legislator at the persistence of time-wasting recreations:

It is ordered, enacted and statuted that what so ever man is found of what degree or condition so ever he be of, playing at quoits or stones but only to shoot in long bows, short crossbows and hurling of darts and spears, to lose at every time so found in doing the same, eight pence and also at no time to use nor occupy the hurling of the little ball with hockey sticks or staves, nor use no handball to play without the walls, but only the great football, on pain of the pains above limited.

THE GOLDEN AGE OF HURLING

The banning of hurling failed. It survived and became a very popular game in the seventeenth and eighteenth centuries, patronised and promoted by many landlords. One such was Baron Purcell of Loughmore, who had a special field for hurling games. According to one report this was located at the Templemore side of Loughmore Castle. Along one side of the field is a low mound. It is said that one of the Baron Purcells was so enamoured of the game of hurling that he kept a private team of hurlers. The field was their playing ground and the mound, which was artificial, served as a kind of grandstand for the spectators. The best hurler in the squad was Londergen, whose favourite feat was to stand at one end of the castle, throw up the ball and strike it with his hurley high over the roof. Quick as lightning, he would rush to the far end of the building and strike the ball back before it reached the ground and so would cause it to pass and repass nine times in all over the castle without ever allowing it to fall to the ground.

SUMMER AND WINTER HURLING

Hurling teams consisted of twenty or more players, and wagers of up to 100 guineas were commonplace. The result depended on who scored the first goal but there would frequently be return challenge matches, and the concept of the 'best of three' was not unknown, nor was the principle of changing ends after a goal had been scored. There was no set size for the field of play, nor of the goals, but the players seem to have been divided into defenders, midfielders and forwards. On many occasions teams wore distinguishing clothing – sashes, belts, caps or ribbons. And the game could be dangerous.

The most common type of game in Leinster and Munster was *camán*, also called summer or Leinster hurling. This was a summer game that used what is now regarded as a typical hurling stick, a broad camán, and a ball of hair or leather that might be lifted with the hand or struck with the stick. This game might be played across country.

It was a different game to *camánacht* or winter hurling, played generally in winter and on a restricted field of play. This resembled hockey or the Scottish game of shinty, in that it used a thin, crooked stick and a hard ball and was played solely with the stick.

JOHN DUNTON'S DESCRIPTION OF HURLING, 1698

And now I think I may say something to you about the sports among the Irish on their holidays. One exercise they use very much is their hurling, which has something in it not unlike the play called Mall. When the cows are casting their hair, they pull it off their backs and with their hands work it into large balls that grow very hard. This ball they use at the hurling which they strike with a stick called a cammaan about three foot and a half in the handle. At the lower end it is crooked and about three inches broad and on this broad part you may sometimes see one of the gamesters carry the ball tossing it for 40 or 50 yards in spite of all the adverse players: and when he is like to lose it, he generally gives it a great stroke to drive it towards the goal. Sometimes if he misses his blow at the ball, he knocks one of the opposers down, at which no resentment is to be shown. They seldom come off with broken heads or shins in which they glory so much. At this sport one parish or barony challenges another; they pick out 10, 12, or 20 players of a side, and the prize is generally a barrel or two of ale, which is brought to the field and drunk off by the victors on the spot, though the vanquished are not without a share too. This commonly is upon some very large plain, the barer the grass the better, and the goals are 200 or 300 yards one from the other: whichever party drives the ball between the other's goal wins the day. Their champions are of the younger and more active among them, and their kindred and mistresses are frequently spectators of their address. Two or three bagpipes attend the conquerors at the barrel's head and then play them out of the field. At some of these meetings two thousand have been present.

A HURLING LANDLORD

The Cosbys were an Elizabethan family that settled in Stradbally, County Laois in 1563. The first of the line was notorious for his cruelty to the Irish. A descendant of his was Dudley Cosby, who died in 1729. His son, Pole, wrote thus about him in his autobiography: 'He danced on the ropes as well as any rope dancer that ever was. He was a fine tennis and five player, a most extraordinary fine hurler and very fond of all those things, and practised them very much when he was young and able.' Dudley Cosby and Nicholas Purcell of Loughmore would have been contemporaries, and the distance between Stradbally and Templemore is not very great. It is conceivable that they had a contest between their estate teams, with a hefty wager on the winner!

ANOTHER DESCRIPTION OF HURLING, C. 1790

Coquebert de Montbret was a Frenchman in the employment of the diplomatic service of the revolutionary French government, who was stationed in Ireland from 1789 to 1791. Writing in the neighbourhood of Loughrea, County Galway, he says:

It is the month of August that the playing of hurley commences. Each team is divided into three groups. The back guard the goal and strive to prevent the ball from passing there. Another group is in front to prevent the enemy's ball from repassing from their side. That is the middle. The third or the whip is on the field between the middle and their opponents' back to force the ball to pass under the goal. The game is played only in Munster and Connacht. In Leinster football is played. In Ulster the Presbyterians are scandalised by Sunday play.

POPULARITY OF HURLING
LEADS TO PITCH INVASION

The *Hibernian Journal* for 17 October 1792 carried a report of a hurling game:

> Yesterday, Tuesday, a hurling match took place in the Phoenix Park, which was honoured by the presence of Her Excellency, the Countess of Westmoreland, and several of the nobility and gentry, besides a vast concourse of spectators. Much agility and athletic contention took place, and great diversion was afforded, until the spectators forced into the playing ground. Colonel Lennox, Nr. Daly and several other gentlemen most obligingly used their endeavours to prevent any interruptions to the players, but to no effect. This active contest ended without either side claiming triumph and remains to be yet decided.

DETAILED ACCOUNT
OF HURLING CONTEST

In 1831, Fr Matt Horgan, the parish priest of Blarney, County Cork wrote the following account of a stirring hurling contest between two teams beside the river Awmartin, a few miles north of Blarney, in 1770. He put it together from conversations he had with some of his parishioners, whose fathers had been eyewitnesses to the event:

> The leaders of the respective teams were Rowland Davies of Dawstown, Blarney, a landlord's son and Denis Horgan of Ballynaraha, in the same parish, who was son to a prosperous farmer. Forty days were required to publish the terms of the impending contest and to assemble the players. Davies invited every hurler from Blarney to the western coast, brought them together and exercised them the day before the day appointed.
> The plain on which the match was fought was by the river Awmartin, a little north-west of Garrycloyne Chapel and

a few miles north of Blarney. The playing field was almost three-quarters of a mile in length, without fence, hollow or slough, surrounded by hills which sloped gently to the verge.

Tents were pitched on both sides of the river, well filled with provisions to feed the spectators and the match was held on a fine day in the month of July, when the grass was dry and short and the ground elastic underfoot.

Davies had his men clad in the most becoming manner. On the head was worn a green cap fringed with a band. A green ribbon bound the collars and wrists of the shirts and a red sash was around the waist. A white trouser was worn but the feet were bare lest any covering on them might retard the speed of the player.

The number of players allowed on each side was fifty and by noon Davies' men were drawn up in order before the tents, whence they marched to the centre of the plain, where they formed into line. The music of the pipes, under a green flag flying, swelled in the gentle breeze. Davies stood at the head dressed in a similar costume to those of his men and distinguished only by his cap which was silk, fringed with deep gold lace and decorated by a feather. He was then about twenty-two years of age and deemed the manly figure in County Cork.

In contrast Horgan contented himself with selecting men from around Cork city and the districts of Whitechurch, Carrignavar and Glenville. They were all well known to him as being youthful, active and well-acquainted with each other from their frequent meetings at local hurling matches. A few famous hurlers from the Youghal and Midleton districts heard of the forthcoming match, offered to try their fortunes and were duly enlisted by him in the team.

Horgan's men were on the eastern side of the little river and at a given signal he marched them on to the field. Their dress was plain, simple and becoming. They were of a hardy appearance, well inured to labour and, seemingly, not discouraged by the splendid appearance of their opponents.

Another signal was sounded and both sides formed with extended lines, having each three divisions. The strongest and ablest men were placed in the main body, consisting of twenty-six men, and the more youthful and active constituted the two wings, twelve on each side. At both extremities of the plain, two lofty poles had been erected, between which the ball should be impelled to decide the victory. The teams, consisting of one hundred handsome looking men, with hurleys in hand, stood facing each other until the plain was cleared.

On casting lots, Horgan won and decided to play facing the southern goalposts, though the sun's rays were shining in their faces. Then the round, elastic, well-covered ball was thrown in and the battle commenced. Both teams flew like lightning to oppose each other and such feats of activity, strength and exertion were never witnesses on that plain.

The two captains were in the midst of the fray and did everything possible to encourage the men. The game continued for two hours and nobody succeeded in obtaining the much coveted goal. Sometimes the men of the east bore the ball south but O'Sullivan from Beara and Healy from the Shoornagh Valley proved invincible. They are described as having the strength of heroes and successfully repelled all attacks.

At length when the players showed signs of exhaustion, Davies called for a cessation. This was granted and all went to their tents for some refreshments. They rested their weary limbs for a time and resumed the game with renewed vigour. The battle became more intense ... The shock of the conflict was tremendous, many were levelled to the ground and the shouts of the spectators ascended to the high heavens, so that it would appear some great battle conflict between the nations was in progress.

The sun was now approaching the western hills and both sides strengthened themselves for the deciding effort. Young Cronin from the Boggeragh watched keenly for a chance and stood at a little distance from his opponent. When the ball came he impelled it before him with such velocity that no enemy could outstrip him until he directed it between the two lofty poles and gained the victory.

Davies was so proud of his team winning that he forgave Horgan the wager. He entertained both sides with their friends at his hospitable mansion from which they departed the next day, each to his own part of the country. Some years later Rowland Davies died in Antigua in the West Indies to the grief of everybody who knew him. The hurleys used on the day, whether broken or whole, were kept by the players during their lives as a memorial of that well-fought struggle on the banks of the Awmartin.

DECLINE IN HURLING

Hurling began to decline towards the end of the eighteenth century and gathered pace during the following century. The cause of this decline had to do with the changing relationship between the landlords and the people, which led to the former abandoning their patronage of the game. There were a number of reasons for this development. It was part of a European phenomenon of the abandonment of popular culture by the nobility. One commentator describes it thus:

The nobles were adopting more 'polished' manners, a new and more self-conscious style of behaviour, modelled on the courtesy books ... Noblemen were learning to exercise self-control, to behave with a studied nonchalance, to cultivate a sense of style and to move in a dignified manner as if engaging in a formal dance ... Noblemen stopped eating in the great halls with their retainers and withdrew into separate dining-rooms ... They stopped wrestling with their peasants, as they used to do in Lombardy, and they stopped killing bulls in public as they used to do in Spain. The noblemen learned to speak and write 'correctly' according to formal rules and to avoid technical terms and the dialect words used by craftsmen and peasants.

Mixing with retainers in a game of hurling was no longer possible; even riding up and down the playing field wielding a whip during the game, keeping the yokels in check, was no longer the done thing. Placing wagers and sharing the barrel of ale after the game would be completely detrimental to the new image.

Another reason for the change was that such gatherings for games of hurling, as advertised in the newspapers, might be suspected of seditious undertones in the changing political climate of the last years of the century. This had come about as a result of Whiteboy activity and later the United Irishmen and the Rising of 1798. The developments in Wexford and the south-east destroyed the political relationship between landlord and tenant. Another aspect was the great slaughter of thousands of men of hurling age in the south-east. The Act of Union and the Napoleonic Wars altered the way of life of many landlords, turning them into absentees and bringing to an end the great days of barony hurling and landlord patronage.

FURTHER DECLINE IN THE NINETEENTH CENTURY

The decline persisted into the nineteenth century. There was the continued withdrawal by the landlords from social involvement with their tenants and the common people, covering the areas of language, manners, attitudes and pastimes. The expanding population began to be seen as a threat to the security of the landlords.

Another factor was the spread of Sunday observance. Gradually the Catholic Church adopted the sabbatarianism of the Protestant churches and began to frown on games on Sunday as something frivolous and a waste of time as well as being occasions for drunkenness, debauchery and sin. As a result the clergy, who might have taken on the leadership role abandoned by the landlords, left the people to fend for themselves.

The Great Famine was a disaster for the national pastimes. The decline in national morale and the destruction of rural society in many areas caused a dramatic decline in traditional pastimes. Twenty years after the event, one commentator recalled the effect of the Famine on the ordinary people: 'Their ancient sports and pastimes everywhere disappeared and in many parts ... have never returned. The outdoor games, the hurling match ... are seen no more.'

Emigration added to the plight of the game so that by the last quarter of the century hurling had almost disappeared. This was one commentator's description of the state of the game in 1883: 'The most of the hurlers are now beyond the Atlantic wave and the remainder go whistling vacantly around the roads at home. Our schoolboys have permanently settled down to cricket, but our farmers' sons no longer interest themselves in the rounding of the boss or the feel of the hockey.'

THE POPULARITY OF CRICKET

In his letter accepting the invitation to become a patron of the new Gaelic Athletic Association, Archbishop Croke expressed his fear of the spread of 'such foreign and fantastic field sports as lawn tennis, polo, croquet, cricket and the like' in Irish life. For him these imports were taking over from 'our own grand national sports'. In his book on cricket in Tipperary, Patrick Bracken provides plenty of evidence that Croke's fears were not fanciful but that cricket was the leading sport in terms of playing numbers from the late 1860s to the early 1880s. The spread of cricket was to be halted by the Land Wars, the absence of a league structure, and, most importantly by the foundation of the Gaelic Athletic Association (GAA). The first cricket club was formed at Carrick-on-Suir in 1834 and it was followed by other clubs in Nenagh, Clonmel, Templemore and Cahir. At this stage the game was very much a minority one between British settlers, landlords and the army, but it was to become much more popular from the 1860s onwards. Bracken shows that Tipperary had at least twenty-nine teams in 1868 and the number was to reach forty-three by the middle of the 1870s. Schools took up the game and many of the rural teams were typically tenant-farmer based. This successful development of the game was to be halted by the efforts of the GAA to restore 'our own grand national sports' and the introduction of the GAA 'ban' in 1902 was to be the death knell of cricket.

DR CROKE'S DESCRIPTION OF THE STATE OF IRELAND

Even more depressing was the description of the state of Irish life given by Dr Croke when he replied to Michael Cusack's request to him to become a patron of the new Gaelic Athletic Association:

... Ball-playing, hurling, football-kicking according to Irish rules, casting, leaping in various ways, wrestling, handy-grips, top-pegging, leap-frog, rounders, tip-in-the-hat and all the favourite exercises and amusements amongst men and boys may now be said to be not only dead and buried but in several localities to be entirely forgotten and unknown ... indeed, if we continue travelling for the next score years in the same direction that we have been going in for some time past condemning the sports that were practised by our fore-fathers, effacing out national features as though we are ashamed of them and putting on, with England's stuffs and broadcloths, her masher habits and such other effeminate follies that she may recommend, we had better, at once and publicly abjure our nationality, clap hands for joy at the sight of the Union Jack and place 'England's red' exultantly above the green.

2

THE FORMATION OF THE GAA

MICHAEL CUSACK

Michael Cusack was the man who better recognised the perilous state of the game of hurling than anyone else at the end of the nineteenth century. Born into an Irish-speaking family in Carron, County Clare in September 1847, he grew up to be a strong athletic young man and played most of the sports of the day. He became a teacher in Dublin and later opened his own school, the Civil Service Academy in Gardiner's Place. He was to make an impression on the young James Joyce, appearing as 'the football fellow in the knickerbockers' in *Stephen Hero*, as 'Michael Cusack the Gael' in *The Portrait of the Artist*, caricatured with the figure 'The Citizen' in *Ulysses* and referred to as 'Sir Micholas de Cusack' in *Finnegan's Wake*.

From his participation in Irish athletics he came to deplore the exclusiveness which debarred workmen from competing. As a result of meeting Pat Nally, a leading nationalist and athlete, Cusack set out to reform Irish athletics. Later, he was to turn his mind to hurling. 'In my dreams I was living with the men of Erin of pre-Christian times. In spirit I hunted and fished with Fionn's invincible hosts from Antrim to Kerry. I hurled with the Fianna of sixteen centuries ago from Tara to Killarney. I resolved to bring back the hurling.'

In December 1882 he founded the Dublin Hurling Club. Hurling, of a sort, had been played in Dublin for some time. There was even an Irish Hurley Union in the city which had at least fourteen clubs. But hurley was not hurling. It was a refined version of the ancient Irish game that persisted in scattered areas throughout the country.

Increasingly, Cusack came to the conclusion that hurley was no substitute for the real thing. His first effort to revive true Irish hurling by founding the Dublin Hurling Club, failed. His second attempt, with the Academy Hurling Club and the Metropolitan Club, was more successful. The Metropolitans became a great success and Cusack, who had formed the club 'to test the pulse of the nation' stepped up his mission to revive hurling.

THE METROPOLITANS *v.* KILLIMOR

One of the few places in the country where the game of hurling had survived was Killimor in south Galway. The earliest set of hurling rules to have been adopted was at a meeting of the Killimor club in February 1885, even though there is a good argument that they were in existence since 1869. When Killimor heard of the revival of hurling by the Metropolitan Club, they issued a challenge to play them. A cup was put up by the people of the town and the Fair Green in Ballinasloe was chosen as the venue.

An advertisement in the *Western Star* screamed: 'Hurling! Hurling! Revival of the National Game'.

The match was arranged for Easter Monday, 13 April 1884. The Midland Railway issued return tickets to the Metropolitan players and their friends to Ballinasloe at the single-fare price.

Before the game started the Killimor captain, F.W. Lynch, and the Metropolitan captain, Michael Cusack, settled the rules of the match. They agreed to play for four half-hours, no tripping or wrestling to be allowed. The winners were to be the team that scored the greater number of goals during the period. The match wasn't a great success. A big crowd turned up, which constantly encroached onto the pitch. In spite of the agreed set of rules, the game was a disappointment and it came to a premature end when Killimor scored a goal.

According to the report in the *Western Star*:

Mr. Cusack lost all heart in the business, and before the second goal was played off stated that his men were not able to the task, but hinted in the blandest manner possible that his opponent's play was too rough, which not one but himself evidently could see, even most of his own men wished to play out but to no use … Mr. Cusack could not be induced to go on, evidently thinking that it would look better before the public to draw off than be beaten badly …

The Galway men claimed victory and this was honoured by bonfires and lights all the way from Ballinasloe to Killimor.

THE NEED TO CONTROL IRISH ATHLETICS

Following his experience at Ballinasloe, Cusack came to realise the need to standardise the rules of play if hurling were to be revived. During the months following the game Cusack argued the need for a new body to govern Irish athletics and wrest from them the control of the Amateur Athletic Association of England. He also saw the need for support from leaders of Church and State. In an anonymous (but clearly from Cusack's pen) article in the *United Ireland* and the *Irishman* on 11 October 1884, entitled 'A Word on Irish Athletics', he argued the point that the social and political development of a nation depended on the cultivation and preservation of its games. Irish athletics were in the hands of people of anti-Irish outlook, who excluded the ordinary person from the sport. Since the best athletes in the country were nationalists, they should take control of their own affairs.

MAURICE DAVIN

One of the people who responded to the article was Maurice Davin of Carrick-on-Suir. He agreed with the views expressed in the article, stated that Irish football and hurling deserved public support and was willing to help any development to revive both games under new rules.

Davin, who was a farmer, was Ireland's most famous athlete at the time. A 'big reachy man', black haired with a full auburn beard, he stood over 6 foot tall and weighed 15 stone. He had dominated Irish athletics during the 1870s. Born in 1842, his first love was boxing but he soon abandoned that in favour of rowing on the river Suir and taking part in regattas. At the age of 29 he began to devote his spare time to weight-throwing, which included shot putting, hammer-throwing and slinging the weights. His brothers, Tom and Pat, also excelled in athletics and in the ten years between 1873 and 1882 between them they won a total of twenty-six Irish national titles and in each event that they contested they set new record figures with one exception. They also represented Ireland in athletic meets with England and Maurice was a victor on a number of occasions. His standing in Ireland as an outstanding athlete had the added prestige that came from having defeated Englishmen.

In his reply to Cusack's 'Word', Davin called for proper rules for football and hurling – 'I would not care to see either game now as the rules stand at present' – and noted that there was still a strong residual love of traditional forms of athletics: 'for one bystander who takes off his coat to run a footrace, forty strip to throw weights or try a jump of some kind.'

THE CHOICE OF THURLES

When Michael Cusack decided to call a meeting for the revival of Gaelic pastimes his first choice wasn't Thurles. Early on he decided against holding it in Dublin and considered Cork as a possible venue. Then Loughrea became his preferred choice. He had got to know of the strong hurling tradition in south-east Galway from his early teaching days in Lough Cultra School, not far from Gort. An indication of the persistence of the game there was the existence of a set of rules, the Killimor Rules, which dated back to 1869. On the basis of the strength of the game in the area, Cusack brought his Metropolitan team to Ballinasloe for a challenge with the local side.

During this visit he got to know the sterling qualities of the Bishop of Clonfert, Dr Patrick Duggan. Later, in August 1884, when the idea of the new organisation was forming in his mind, he realised that its success would depend on powerful patrons.

Dr Duggan was then 71 years of age and had already offered his resignation to the Pope because of his rather poor health. However, he was delighted to hear of the founding of the Association and promised to do all he could to promote its success. But he declined to act as patron and advised Cusack to ask Dr Croke, Archbishop of Cashel, 'a fine Gael, young, vigorous and energetic' to become the first patron of the new body. And so, Cusack came to Thurles and the rest is history.

THE INVITATION

Michael Cusack was sufficiently satisfied with the response to his article 'A Word on Irish Athletics' and decided to hold a meeting at Thurles on 1 November 1884:

> 4,Gardiner Place,
> Dublin.
> October 27, 1884.
>
> Dear Sir: You are earnestly requested to attend a meeting which will be held at Thurles on the 1st of November to take steps for the formation of a Gaelic Association for the preservation and cultivation of our National Pastimes and for providing rational amusement for Irish people during their leisure hours. The movement which it is proposed to inaugurate has been approved by Mr. Michael Davitt, Mr. Justin McCarthy, M.P., Mr. William O'Brien, M.P., Mr. T. Harrington, M.P. and other eminent men who are interested in the social elevation of the race. The place of meeting will be decided upon at the Commercial Hotel, Thurles, at 2 o'clock on the day of the meeting.
> Signed: Maurice Davin, Carrick-on-Suir
> Michael Cusack, Dublin, hon. Sec. pro tem.
> N.B. – the favour of a reply is requested – Michael Cusack

THE MEETING

The meeting took place in the Commercial Hotel, Thurles, which was owned by Miss Lizzie Hayes.

It proved fully capable of accommodating all who turned up. Indeed, when the meeting commenced at about 3 p.m., the billiard room sufficed. The exact number present is in dispute. Seven founding fathers are officially recognised. Cusack later indicated that nine persons were present. A study of contemporary newspaper accounts gives a figure as high as fourteen. As well as those present a substantial number of apologies was received as well as messages of support for the new organisation. In all they numbered about sixty, some from as far afield as Australia and America.

THE FOUNDING FATHERS

The seven official founders were as follows:

- Michael Cusack from Carron, County Clare, a teacher
- Maurice Davin from Carrick-on-Suir, County Tipperary, a farmer
- John Wyse Power, a journalist, editor of the *Leinster Leader* and an 'associate of the extreme section of Irish Nationalism'
- James K. Bracken, a building contractor and a monumental mason from Templemore, County Tipperary, who was a prominent member of the Irish Republican Brotherhood
- Joseph P. O'Ryan, who was born in Carrick-on-Suir and practised as a solicitor in Callan and Thurles
- John McKay, a Belfast man then working as a journalist with the *Cork Examiner*
- District Inspector St George McCarthy, who was born in Bansha, County Tipperary and who was a member of the Royal Irish Constabulary stationed at Templemore

THE UNOFFICIAL LIST

As well as the official founders a number of other people are reputed to have been present at the meeting. They include Frank Moloney from Nenagh, William Foley from Carrick-on-Suir and Thurles residents T.K. Dwyer, Charles Culhane, William Delahunty, John Butler and Michael Cantwell. There is a strong Kilkenny tradition that Henry Joseph Meagher, father of the famous Lory, Jack Hoyne, who played on Kilkenny's first All-Ireland winning side in 1904, and a third Tullaroan man, Ned Teehan, also attended the foundation meeting.

DECISIONS TAKEN

Officers elected were Maurice Davin as chairman and Michael Cusack, John McKay and John Wyse Power as joint secretaries.

The new Association was named 'The Gaelic Athletic Association for the Preservation and Cultivation of National Pastimes.'

It was agreed to invite Charles Stewart Parnell, Archbishop Croke of Cashel & Emly and Michael Davitt to become Patrons of the new Association.

The new officers were requested to draw up rules for the Association.

THE PATRONS ACCEPT

Having patrons was very important for any organisation and the choice of Croke, Davitt and Parnell as patrons represented recognition of the major forces in the Irish nationalist movement of the day. They all readily accepted.

In the course of his reply, Dr Croke accepted 'with the utmost pleasure.'

In his reply Charles Stewart Parnell stated that he felt 'very much honoured by the resolution adopted at the Thurles meeting and I accept with appreciation the position of patron of the Association which has been offered to me. I need not say that I shall do anything I can to render the working of the movement a success.'

Michael Davitt had already written to Cusack expressing his regrets for being unable to attend the foundation meeting. Now, in accepting the position of patron, he promised to do anything 'it is in my power to do to further the objects of the Association' and reiterated 'my entire sympathy with the objects of the Gaelic Athletic Association.'

A BRASH AND OPINIONATED MAN

Michael Cusack was the man mostly responsible for the foundation of the Gaelic Athletic Association. Without him the Association would never have come into existence. Once he 'discovered' hurling at the end of 1882 his mission became to re-establish the national game.

His 'conversion' to the game was unheralded and complete. Prior to the end of 1882 he was devoted to cricket and rugby and was a typical all-round sportsman in that he played handball, rowed and took part in athletics.

He was a well-known and prominent figure around Dublin through his sporting endeavours and also through the success of his Academy in Gardiner Place, which he set up in 1877. This became an immediate success in preparing boys for the civil service. Interestingly, in the light of later events, one of his students was Thomas St George McCarthy.

But Cusack was more than a successful sportsman and educator. According to historian Paul Rouse, he 'had already cultivated an idiosyncratic appearance that allowed him to stand out from the crowd. He walked through the city in heavy working boots, a blackthorn stick swinging from his arm, and with a heavy frieze coat covering his heavy-set, broad-shouldered frame. His full black beard was beginning to streak with grey. Overall, he was remarkably proud and self-conscious of his appearance, which seems not so much to have been a mark of eccentricity but a statement of defiance. He gloried in the idea of his distinctiveness, the idea that he was a singular man, of singular beliefs. And he used the rapidly developing world of the Dublin press to broadcast these beliefs.'

Cusack was also a noted journalist and contributed to papers on a wide range of issues. He used the press to propagate his opinions on athletics and also to promote the revival of hurling. Once the GAA was founded he used his journalistic skills to build momentum in favour of the new Association.

The founding of the GAA was the high point, the outstanding achievement of Michael Cusack's life. Unfortunately everything was downhill after that. An opinionated and combative individual he was incapable of diplomacy and in his personal and journalistic statements preferred the bludgeon to the sword.

He fell out with Archbishop Croke and Michael Davitt and alienated virtually every section of the GAA within eighteen months of its foundation. Eventually he succeeded in having himself ejected from the organisation. Following his ejection, William O'Brien, the owner of the *United Ireland*, a paper which had been a major platform for Cusack's view, dispensed with his services.

Following this setback Cusack founded the *Celtic Times* in January 1887. The masthead read 'Let native industries, literature, arts and pastimes flourish.' The paper covered every aspect of Irish life but the new Gaelic Athletic Association was its major focus. Sports coverage was a new phenomenon and the *Celtic Times* carried many match reports from around the country. Cusack also used its columns to attack those he regarded as the enemies of the Association and those who had caused him to be ejected. Unfortunately, the paper lacked backers and folded in January 1888.

Cusack's final sixteen years are rather sad. He earned a precarious existence from journalism and teaching, in contrast to the £1,500 a year he was reputed to be earning at the time of the foundation of the GAA. His wife, Margaret Wood, died from TB in 1890 and one of his daughters, Mary, aged 8, died a month later. The rest of the children were scattered to relatives and two of his sons to an orphanage in Glasnevin. Perhaps to overcome his frustration, Cusack occasionally went on heavy drinking bouts. He died suddenly on 28 November 1906 and is buried in Glasnevin cemetery.

THE DEMOCRATISATION OF SPORT

The main business of the new Association was the revival of hurling and the invention of Gaelic football. Even more important was the democratisation of the new sport. Prior to the foundation of the GAA participation in sport was elitist, a pastime for the upper and leisured classes. In fact many sports denied participation to anyone who worked with his hands. All this was to change, and change utterly, with the opening up of athletics, hurling, football, handball, rounders etc. to all comers. The humblest man in society had an equal right with the landlord to participate.

No wonder then that the GAA, in Cusack's description, 'spread like a prairie fire'. The Irish national pastimes were opened up to the massive ranks of the previously disenfranchised. This led to the huge proliferation in the formation of clubs soon after the foundation of the GAA.

BIG SPORTS MEETINGS

During the early years the GAA was essentially an athletics body, promoting big sports meeting throughout the country. The first of these was in Clonmel in February 1885 and following that there was a succession of very successful and well-attended meetings around the country. Field events, which weren't given the same recognition under Amateur Athletic Association and Irish Amateur Athletic Association rules, came into their own. The competitive aspect of these meetings appealed to people as local heroes received the recognition denied them in the past. There was enormous enthusiasm, because the great majority of those participating were doing so for the first time.

THE RULES OF THE GAME

At the second meeting of the new organisation, held in Cork on 27 December 1884, the rules for hurling, football, weight-throwing and jumping were discussed and adopted. Rules for running, walking and bicycle events were also approved.

Some of the early games of hurling were prone to violence and pitch invasions and the decisions of referees were often contested, with teams occasionally walking off the field in disagreement. It was therefore decided that there should be two umpires and a referee. When the umpires disagreed, the referee's decision was to be final. There should be an umpire at each goal to watch the goals and the points. The referee should be the timekeeper and throw in the ball at the commencement of each game.

Other rules included the size of the ground, which should be at least 196 yards by 140 yards. There shouldn't be less than fourteen or more than twenty-one players aside. The goal posts were to be 21 feet apart with the crossbar 10½ feet from the ground. Beside the goal posts, side point posts were to be provided.

Goals were the only scores allowed in the early days; later the point was to be introduced for the ball going over the crossbar. There was also a 'forfeit point', awarded if a defender carried the ball over the goal line. This was to disappear after 1886, when side posts were introduced. If a player hit a ball between the side posts, this registered as a point. During the early years a goal had no equivalent in points. After some years 5 points, and later 3, were declared equal to a goal. Play was limited to an hour's duration after 1886. The match should be decided by the greater number of goals, and where no goals were made, or where an equal number were scored, by the greater number of points.

The ball should not be less than 4½ inches or more than 5 inches in diameter, and should not weigh less than 7 ounces or more than 10 ounces. A ball made of cork and woollen thread, and covered in leather, was recommended to players. The hurley might be of any pattern fancied by the player.

Sides were to change ends at half-time in a game. The umpires or referee were to throw in the ball when it got out of play, except when it crossed the end lines, when it was pucked out from the goal posts. The ball must not be lifted off the ground by the hands when in play. It might be struck with the hand or kicked. It might be caught in the hand when off the ground and pucked in any way the player wished, but it must not be carried or thrown.

When the rules were broken the referee might allow a free. In free pucks the ball must not be taken in the hand. If the ball struck a bystander, near the sidelines, except the referee or the umpire, it was out of play and thrown in by one of the officials.

A player should not catch, trip or push from behind, or bring his hurley intentionally into contact with another player. For each breach of this rule the referee was empowered to suspend the player for the game and allow no substitute in his place. If a player was hurt as a result of a breach of this rule, the referee should allow a substitute. He could also award a free.

One of the most unusual of the new rules was that wrestling was permitted. Two players came into contact and immediately got into a physical tussle. Only one fall was allowed. If the players attempted a second fall on the same occasion, the referee intervened. While the players were wrestling the remainder of their teammates got on with the game.

THE PARISH RULE

One of the most important decisions taken at the Cork meeting was the adoption of the 'Parish Rule', the principle of one club for each parish and the confinement of each native to his own parish for playing purposes. The parish was a unit its inhabitants could identify with. This territorial identification, as well as being a great bonding force for club teams in the early years, was to be strengthened when neighbouring parishes, and later counties, were pitted against each other. Dr Kevin Whelan has drawn attention to this phenomenon by quoting the painter Tony O'Malley, who contrasted the tribal-territorial element in Irish sport with English attitudes. 'If neighbours were playing, like New Ross and Tullogher, there would be a real needle in it. When Carrickshock were playing I once heard an old man shouting, "Come on the men that bate the procters," and there was a tremor and a real fervour in his voice. It was a battle cry, with the hurleys as the swords, but with the same intensity.' Whelan continues: 'Similar forces of territoriality have been identified behind the success of cricket in the West Indies and rugby in the Welsh valleys.'

This territorial allegiance was reinforced by the adoption of club colours, often drawn from the old faction favours. Clubs and counties have become so identified with their colours that one couldn't imagine Cork without their red jerseys or Kilkenny in anything but their stripy black and amber. The colours seem to tell one something about the team and give a shape and attitude to the players in them. The same colours, while giving a feeling of identification to followers of the team, can also excite feelings of fear, antagonism and even hate in the minds of their opponents.

As well as some of the colours being inherited from the days of the faction fights, an occasional faction slogan has been carried over too. 'If any man can, an Alley man can.' 'Squeeze 'em up Moycarkey, and hang 'em out to dry.' Lingering animosities can sometimes surface in surprising ways: it is not unknown for an irate Wexford supporter to hurl abuse at Kilkenny, recalling an incident that occurred in Castlecomer to indignant United Irishmen in 1798: 'Sure what good are they anyway? Didn't they piss on the powder in '98?'

FIRST INTER-COUNTY HURLING MATCH

Inter-county matches didn't take place until 1886 and one of the first was played in the Phoenix Park between North Tipperary and South Galway on 16 February. It reflected the advent of authoritative rules for hurling and that the games could now be organised at a wider level. Prior to this time all hurling rules were local and prevented the game being organised outside a local area, unless there was agreement between the two teams on the rules.

The man responsible for organising the game was 'Mr Hurling' himself, Michael Cusack, and he was keen to spread the gospel of hurling. His contact in Tipperary was Frank Moloney, the secretary of Nenagh Hurling Club, and he would have been familiar with the strength of the game in Galway from his time teaching there.

The two teams travelled by train to Dublin the previous day and met up at Broadstone Station at 10 p.m. They spent the night in the Clarence Hotel and received instructions on the rules of play. The players marched out to the field the following day.

The 15 acres in the Phoenix Park was the venue for the game and it had been laid out and was stewarded by members of the Dublin and Wicklow clubs. Cusack was the referee and the game lasted eighty minutes. There was a silver cup and twenty-one silver medals for the winners.

To begin the match, an arch of hurleys was formed by the teams facing each other. The Tipperary ball was used for the first half. For forty minutes the game waxed fast and furious, during which the Tipperary men drove twenty-six wides and resisted every attempt by Galway to transfer the sphere of operations to the other end. In the second half the Galway ball, which was smaller, was introduced. The play was less one-sided but the Galway team failed to make an impression on Tipperary. After about twenty minutes a great Tipperary attack, spearheaded by Charles McSorley of the Silvermines, resulted in a goal and deafening cheers from the crowd. During the remaining twenty minutes Galway made some brilliant dashes but to no avail and the final whistle left Tipperary victorious by a solitary goal.

The cup and the medals were presented to the victorious side by Mrs Fitzgerald, then Lady Mayoress of Dublin. The Tipperary team were given a torchlight procession on their return to Nenagh and about 4,000 people turned up in front of the Castle Hotel to listen to Frank Moloney's address.

(The match is regarded in some quarters as the first unofficial All-Ireland final. At any rate the cup is the oldest GAA trophy and is to be found in Lár na Páirce, Thurles.)

3

THE FIRST ALL-IRELAND CHAMPIONSHIP

Local rivalries between parishes gradually evolved into county identifications. The first inter-county championship was inaugurated in 1887. The following rules governed the championship:

- It would be open to all affiliated clubs in the GAA, all entries to be made on or before 1 January each year. Each team to pay an entrance fee of 2s 6d
- Clubs in the county had to play the ties out first and the winner of the final tie would be entitled to play for the championship
- The first ties were to be played on such days and venues as the County Committee appointed, but no sooner than 1 February or later than 17 March, and the final ties at such times and places as the Executive appointed
- The first match was to be played on the last week of April or the first week of May. The winning team and the second were to receive championship medals of the GAA. A player was not allowed to play for more than one club in the championship
- The number of players a side in each of the matches was to be 21

FIVE OUT OF TWELVE

Twelve teams entered the inaugural All-Ireland hurling championship but only five participated. Galway, represented by the Meelick Club, defeated Wexford, represented by Castlebridge, by 2-8 to 1-0. Ten thousand people turned up for the match at Elm Park, Dublin on 24 July 1887. According to one reporter, 'There was a good deal of heated temper on both sides. The conduct of the Wexford men was severely censured by most of those present. One incident of the day's proceedings cannot be too highly valued. Lord French, when he heard of the great victory of Galway, directed his steward, Mr Balfe, to go to the Midland Hotel and hand from him £3 to treat the team and also £2 to one of the team that had lost two teeth by a blow of the hurl.'

Tipperary, represented by Thurles, got a walkover from Dublin, whose application for a postponement on the grounds that some of their players were on holiday was refused, and beat Clare at Nenagh by 1-7 to 0-2. Afterwards they beat Kilkenny, represented by Tullaroan, at Urlingford by 4-7 to 0-0.

THE FINAL

The final wasn't played until 1 April 1888. The venue was Hoare's field in Birr, quite close to the present hurling field, and the referee was Patrick White from Toomevara, County Tipperary, who was then working at Birr. The Galway (Meelick) team consisted of twelve men from Meelick and nine from Killimor. The two parishes joined up as a result of three games they had played against each other the year before the championship. The games ended in draws and as the teams couldn't beat one another they decided to combine.

The Meelick men on the team were Pat Madden, who was the captain and one of the famous Maddens from the locality, Patrick Cullen, Mike Manning, John Colohan, John Scally, Willie Madden, Tom Hanley, James Kelly, Pat Manning, Jin Connolly, John Cosgrave and Arthur Cosgrave. The Killimor men were John Lowry, John Callinan, Pat Haverty, Tom Foley, Owen Griffin, Patrick Larkin, John Manning, Charlie Melody and John Sanders.

FENIANS ONLY!

According to local tradition, only Fenians could get on the team. One fine player in the area, named Burke, failed to get selected for this reason. The hurleys for the final were made on the kitchen floor of Patrick Cullen's house. Cullen was a carpenter who was to flee to American in 1891 as a result of land trouble in the locality. He was never to return.

The team travelled to the final by McIntyre's brake, with the exception of John Lowry, who walked all the way from Killimor to Birr. When they arrived they heard that Tipperary weren't going to appear. It is claimed in some quarters that this was a rumour put out by the Tipperary men to get Meelick off guard, but it may have originated because of disagreement in the Tipperary camp. Whatever the reason the Galway men went for a drink and while imbibing heard that Tipperary were ready.

DISPUTE ABOUT EXPENSES

There was a dispute in the Tipperary camp that day and it was about expenses. The captain, Denis Maher, and six of the Killinan players didn't travel to the match. They had requested the county committee to pay their expenses to Birr, because of the costs incurred in travelling to Nenagh, Clonmel and Urlingford for the earlier rounds. The committee didn't agree and, in the words of the aggrieved captain, 'there were men from Gortnahoe, Drombane and Moyne called in and their expenses paid and seven of the old hurlers left standing on the platform, namely D. Maher, Jack Maher, Conn Callanan, Pat Ryan, Matty Maher, Ned Maher and myself.'

The actual selection was as follows: Jim Stapleton (capt.), Matty Maher, Andy Maher, Tom Bourke, Ned Murphy, Tom Stapleton, Ger Dwyer, Mick Carroll, Tom Carroll, Tom Maher, John Leamy, Ned Lambe, Martin McNamara, John Mockler, Ger Ryan, Danny Ryan, Tom Dwyer, Ned Bowe, Tommy Healy, Jim Leahy, Johnny

Dunne. The players came from the following clubs, Thurles, Two-Mile-Borris, The Ragg, Moyne, Gortnahoe and Drombane.

PLAYED IN SHIRTS AND TROUSERS

Both teams togged out in Cunningham's Hotel and then marched to the field. Togging out is probably a misnomer as it is generally accepted that the Galway men played in their shirts and trousers and each player wore a green knitted cap with a tassel on it. Meelick were led by their non-playing captain, James Lynam, who had held the military rank of captain in the American Civil War. Although a noted pugilist, he was counted a quiet man. His family came from Rahan, County Offaly, and he had a farm in Eyrecourt. Later, in the 1890s, he was to contest unsuccessfully the East Galway seat in the Parnellite interest against John Roche MP.

The game was fought at a fierce pace. One of the Thurles players got a blow to the nose and had to be carried off. As a result, John Lowry, who had walked to Birr and played at full-back for Killimor, was taken off by Captain Lynam. He was none too pleased with the decision because, for some time thereafter, until he was warned by the referee, he would dart onto the field and take part in the play. Thurles won by a goal, scored by Tommy Healy of Two-Mile-Borris, and a point and one forfeit point to nil.

4

EARLY CHAMPIONSHIP SUCCESSES

DUBLIN WIN FIRST ALL-IRELAND

No All-Ireland hurling final was played in 1888 because of the so-called 'American Invasion', when a number of athletes and hurlers travelled to the United States to publicise the Gaelic Athletic Association and raise some badly needed funds. On both counts the trip was a failure.

The All-Ireland championship resumed in 1889 and the final was won by a team from Dublin for the first time. The club, Kickhams, represented Dublin and they defeated Clare, represented by Tulla, by 5-1 to 1-6. Clare were favourites going into the game and led by 1-5 to 1-0 at the interval but Dublin dominated the second half. Played at Inchicore on 3 November before 1,500 spectators, the field was extremely wet, which didn't help Clare's chances as they played in their bare feet! Maybe the referee was also a problem as he was P. Tobin, a member of the Dublin County Committee. However, the match finished amicably enough and the Clare team were treated to dinner by the Dublin committee.

MOSTLY FROM TIPPERARY

Dublin's first All-Ireland team was comprised entirely of players born outside the capital. Ten were from Tipperary including the captain, Nicholas O'Shea, who typified the all-round athlete of the early GAA, being also a champion high jumper, pole vaulter and hurdler. Another Tipperary man, Willie Spain, became the first player to win All-Ireland medals in both hurling and football, having won an All-Ireland football medal with Limerick in 1888. Apart from Tipperary's representatives, Kickhams had players from Clare (three) and one each from Kilkenny, Wicklow, Meath, Laois, Longford and Cork.

The captain of the Clare team was John Considine, but he didn't play. This was often the practise in the early days of the GAA when captains were sometimes non-playing members. They were selected owing to their influence in keeping the teams together and making them practice.

CORK WERE 'AWARDED' THEIR FIRST ALL-IRELAND

Cork played Wexford (Castlebridge) in the 1890 All-Ireland final at Clonturk Park, Dublin before 1,000 spectators on 16 November. According to one report the match was very rough and the Castlebridge men played a reckless game with the result that several of the Aghabullogue players were knocked out of action. The Corkmen played in their bare feet and were faster and the more skilful hurlers. At half-time they led by 1-3 to 0-1. In the second half the game became rougher and, with the permission of the referee, John Sheehy, from Limerick, the Aghabullogue captain, withdrew his men from the field when they were leading by 1-6 to 2-2. The match was awarded to Cork following a vote of 3-2 by the Central Council.

The Wexford point of view puts a different slant on the matter. In the vote to award the game it claims that the three delegates who voted in favour of Cork weren't at the match, while the two who wanted a replay, were! It goes on to state that the trouble started when a Corkman lay down and started to moan and a second player followed suit. The Wexford umpire made out they were faking injuries but the referee wouldn't give a decision. Later, though, he advised the Central Council to award the match to

Aghabullogue because of the roughness of the Castlebridge men. He said that seven of the Cork players had to retire. The Wexford people thought it was an absurd decision by the referee, who did not censure anyone while the game lasted. However, Cork were awarded the match.

KERRY WON THEIR ONLY HURLING ALL-IRELAND IN 1891

Kerry, represented by Ballyduff, won their only All-Ireland when they defeated Wexford (Crossabeg) in the 1891 final played at Clonturk Park, Dublin on 28 February 1892, with P. Tobin, who refereed the second All-Ireland, in charge of the game. Two thousand spectators attended the match, which was described as a splendid example of 'muscular hurling'. At the end of the hour the official score stood at 1 goal and 1 point each, and a third half-hour was played, the first and only occasion that extra time was played in a final. Kerry, who played in their bare feet, won by 2-3 to 1-5, but in most unusual circumstances.

At the end of normal time Wexford had scored a point from a free but it was disallowed by the referee because the ball hadn't crossed the Kerry crossbar when the final whistle was blown. He said he had no power to extend the time beyond the hour and had blown the final whistle between the striking of the ball and it going over the bar! The Wexford players were none too pleased and were reluctant to take the field for the extra half-hour. They only did so when the referee threatened to award the game to Kerry. The game was the last to be played with 21 aside. From then on until 1913 teams were made up of 17 a side.

CORK WIN FIRST THREE-IN-A-ROW 1892-94

Cork (Redmonds) defeated Dublin (Flag-Davitts) by 2-4 to 1-1 in the 1892 final played before 5,000 spectators at Clonturk Park, Dublin on 26 March 1893. The game was described as not being up to the standard for an All-Ireland final. It ended in confusion when Dublin withdrew after fifty minutes because the referee allowed a disputed Cork goal to stand. The Central Council later awarded the match to Cork. As well as limiting teams to seventeen players, 5 points were now equal to 1 goal and the county champions were permitted to select the best players in the county, rather than limit their pick to their own club.

Cork (Blackrock) defeated Kilkenny (Confederation) by 6-8 to 0-2 in the 1893 final, which was fixed for the Ashtown Trotting and Athletic Grounds, Phoenix Park on 24 June 1894. According to a newspaper report, the arrangements for the game were very defective with the grass so long that the spectators ripped up the goalposts and re-erected them elsewhere in the park. Admission was sixpence and the attendance is given as 1,000 spectators. The Cork side had an easy victory, having led by 3-4 to 0-1 at the interval. One of the umpires was James Nowlan, later to become president of the GAA, after whom Nowlan Park, Kilkenny is named.

Cork (Blackrock) made it three-in-a-row when they defeated Dublin (Rapparees) by 5-20 to 2-0 in the 1894 final played at Clonturk Park, Dublin on 24 March 1895. Under the new rule whereby the county champions could draft in players from the rest of the county, Rapparees called in three players from the newly formed Celtic club for the final. However, the Rapparees players objected to two of them and permitted only Michael Kelly to play with them. Following their victory, the Cork county board presented a set of medals to Blackrock as All-Ireland Hurling Champions, which may suggest that in the early days it was up to the county board to provide the All-Ireland medals.

FAMED TUBBERADORA

Tubberadora, referred to locally at the 'Golden Square Mile', is a townland at the end of the parish of Boherlahan-Dualla, on the road between Cashel and Thurles. Its claim to fame is based on three All-Irelands won by the club in 1895, 1896 and 1898.

Tipperary (Tubberadora) defeated Kilkenny by 6-8 to 1-0 in the 1895 final, which was played at 'The City and Suburban Grounds', Jones's Road on 15 March 1896, the first final to be played at what later became known as Croke Park. About 6,000 spectators attended the game, the biggest crowd yet at an All-Ireland. In this game umpires used colour flags to indicate scores for the first time in an All-Ireland final.

Tubberadora won their second All-Ireland in 1896, which didn't take place until 27 March 1898. It was also played at Jones's Road and Tipperary defeated Dublin (Commercials) by 8-14 to 0-4. 'Commercials,' wrote Tipperary GAA historian, Canon Fogarty, 'perished like the flowers of spring before the biting winds of March.' The Scanlan brothers, natives of Tubberadora, but then domiciled in Dublin and members of the Commercials team, would not turn out against their old comrades, who included brother Phil, in the final.

Tubberadora did not compete in the 1897 championship because one of their players, John Maher, broke his leg in a clash while practising for a county championship game. So upset were the team that their captain, Mikey Maher, requested and was granted permission to withdraw from the championship.

They had to be persuaded to play in the 1898 championship and went on to win their third All-Ireland when they defeated Kilkenny (Threecastles) by 7-13 to 3-10 in the final, which was played at Jones's Road on 25 March 1900. The Tipperary champions had prepared by practising in Walsh's kiln field in Tubberadora, playing backs and forwards, and the latter improved their shooting prowess through the iron band of a cartwheel.

Tipperary led by 3-4 to 2-4 at half-time but took control in the second half. A big talking point after the game was allowing a Tipperary point made with the hand. At the time such scores weren't allowed. The victorious team was photographed after the game and later entertained to dinner at the Abbey Hotel by a number of Tipperary men resident in the city. For the photograph the team wore the new set of gear presented to them by the Tipperary

Grocers' Assistants residing in Dublin at the beginning of the 1897 championship. It consisted of a navy blue cap, a blue jersey with a yellow sash and navy blue togs.

Following victory in their third All-Ireland the club retired from the fray having won everything that needed to be won and established a permanent place in the history of hurling. From their formation in 1895 Tubberadora had played in fourteen championship matches and their total score was 71 goals and 108 points, while conceding 17 goals and 46 points. Although they went out of existence as a club, many of the players went on to play with neighbouring clubs and win further honours in later years.

PADDY RIORDAN'S RECORD

Paddy Riordan of Rosmult in the parish of Upperchurch-Drombane holds the record for the highest score in an All-Ireland hurling final. In the 1895 final with Tipperary (Tubberadora) he scored all the 6 goals 8 points for the winners. He also holds the record as the only player in an All-Ireland to score all his side's total.

At a time when teams included seventeen players, one played alone on the inside forward line and this was Paddy Riordan's position. Add to that his skill as a hurler and his size at 6 foot 1 inches tall and weighing 13½ stone and he was obviously a formidable forward.

The *Cashel Sentinel* reported his achievement in the 1895 final thus: 'P. Riordan, who was extreme forward, played a grand game. He is a perfect machine in the art of scoring and never lost an opportunity in making the most of his chances.'

TWO ALL-IRELANDS ON THE SAME DAY

There was a second achievement for the Riordan family on the day of the final, which was played on 15 March 1896. Paddy's younger brother, Jim, played with Tipperary (Arravale Rovers) against Meath (Navan O'Mahony's) in the All-Ireland football final on the same day and won, to establish another record of being the only brothers to win All-Irelands in different codes on the same day. In fact the same player transferred to Limerick and, playing with Commercials, won a second All-Ireland football medal in the 1896 All-Ireland.

Paddy Riordan travelled to Stamford Bridge in 1896 and played with Munster, who togged out in royal blue shirts with three gold crowns, navy blue knickers, white caps and shoes, against Leinster as part of the so-called 'Gaelic Invasion of England'. Later he played with Thurles Blues and won a second All-Ireland hurling medal in 1906.

He emigrated to the US in 1908 and three years later led a team of hurlers from New York to play exhibition games in Ireland. He died in New York in February 1941 and was buried in Long Island. His brother, Jim, died two months later and was buried in Limerick.

THE CROKE CUP

The patron of the GAA, Archbishop Croke of Cashel & Emly, celebrated his episcopal silver jubilee on 18 July 1895. In honour of the occasion he presented the eponymous silver cup to the Association and it became the trophy for a secondary hurling competition. It was played for the first time in 1896 and won by Clare (Tulla) who defeated Wexford (Crosstown) by 6 goals 16 points in the final at Jones's Road on 27 June 1897. One newspaper account stated that 'the Wexford players were fairly outpaced by the Banner County men, whose dexterity was simply marvellous, and whose speed was sustained to the end. The victors scored goals and points with machine-like regularity.'

Clare defeated Tubberadora in the Munster final of the competition and they have the distinction of being the only team to beat the famed team during their glorious run of success. In fact, they caused consternation by beating the Tipperary men by 2-3 to 1-3. One reason for the defeat is given by Canon Fogarty in his history of the GAA in Tipperary: 'Mikey Maher took only a reconnoitring party' – the old story of not respecting the opposition!

Tubberadora tried to reverse the result by lodging an objection. The captain, Mikey Maher, and one of the players, Will Devane, gave evidence that at one period of the game they counted an extra player on the Clare (Tulla) side, and when they informed the referee a Tulla player was seen disappearing into the crowd. The objection failed.

The Croke Cup competition was played for a number of years as a prelude to the All-Ireland championship. Later it was combined with the championship and finally disappeared off the GAA program. The cup, however, is still in use and is presented annually to the National Hurling League winners.

CROKE PARK

The Gaelic Athletic Association's premier grounds are named after Archbishop Thomas Croke (1823-1902). The site was originally named the City and Suburban Racecourse and owned by Maurice Butterly. From the closing years of the nineteenth century the grounds were leased for sporting events. The 1895 All-Ireland final was the first major GAA game to be played there and the All-Irelands of 1896, 1897, 1898, 1899, 1901 and 1903 were played there before Frank Dineen, Ballylanders, County Limerick, a former president and secretary of the Association, and a journalist by profession, purchased it for £3,250 in 1908. He held it in trust for the GAA until it could afford to purchase it.

However, he had to sell four acres of it to the Jesuits in 1910, when he had some difficulty funding his bank loan. This land was purchased by the GAA when it commenced its modern re-development of Croke Park towards the end of the twentieth century.

In 1913, a football tournament to raise funds for a Croke Memorial at Thurles realised almost £2,000. This unexpected windfall enabled the Association to purchase the Jones's Road grounds from Frank Dineen for £3,500 and immediately name it Croke Park.

However, the Tipperary county board were upset that funds raised for the Croke Memorial at Thurles were diverted to the purchase and a good old row ensued. The matter was resolved when both Munster and Central Councils gave an additional £200 each to the fund, which brought the total grant for the project to £1,000. The Croke Memorial in Liberty Square was built in 1922. It is a bronze, life-size figure of Archbishop Croke, by Londoner F. Doyle Jones, mounted on a tapering, triangular limestone pedestal.

LIMERICK WIN FIRST ALL-IRELAND

Limerick (Kilfinane) won their first All-Ireland hurling title in the 1897 final when they defeated Kilkenny (Tullaroan) by 3-4 to 2-4 at Tipperary Town on 20 November 1898. Before a crowd of about 5,000 spectators, Kilkenny had the better of the exchanges in the first half and led by 2-4 to 1-1 at the interval. Limerick dominated the second half, prevented Kilkenny from scoring and added 2-3 to their total to win by 3-4 to 2-4. Denis Grimes was the captain of the victorious side and the other Kilfinane men were James 'Sean Óg' Hanley, Maurice and Paddy Flynn, Mick and Jim Finn, Paddy 'Long' O'Brien, Tom 'Goatee' Brazill and Mick Downes. The remaining players were from Cappamore (4) Ballingarry (2), Caherline (1) and Croom (1).

When the All-Ireland champions returned from Tipperary every window of every house in Kilfinane was ablaze with candles, tar barrels blazed on the moat, there were bands everywhere and the celebrations went on into the early hours of the morning.

Limerick had a second great win that year when they won the Croke Cup competition also. They again defeated Kilkenny (Tullaroan) by 3-8 to 1-4 in the final, which was played at Thurles on 9 July 1899. Archbishop Croke attended the match and the teams were presented to him by Frank Dineen, a Limerick man and secretary of the GAA, before the game. He imparted his blessing to the kneeling players.

TWO MORE FOR TIPPERARY

Tipperary teams, Horse & Jockey and Two-Mile-Borris from the parish of Moycarkey, won the 1899 and 1900 All-Irelands. At the time the famed hurling townsland of Tubberadora, which had won the 1895, 1896 and 1898 All-Irelands, was also in the parish and didn't become part of the parish of Boherlahan-Dualla until 1903.

The final of 1899 wasn't played until 24 March 1901 and it was contested by Horse & Jockey and Wexford (Blackwater) before 4,000 spectators at Jones's Road. The game was a close contest in the first half at the end of which Tipperary were ahead by 2-6 to 1-3, but it was one-way traffic in the second half with the Tipperary champions winning easily by 3-12 to 1-4. The last few minutes of the game weren't played as Wexford had no replacement for an injured player. Ten of the victorious side, Tim Condon (capt.), Dick and Jim O'Keeffe, Mike Wall, Watty Dunne, Mikey Maher, Denis and Johnny Walsh, Tommy Ryan and Phil Byrne, had played with Tubberadora.

MICHAEL CUSACK ATTENDS RECEPTION

Blackwater were the first Wexford club to affiliate to the county board in November 1884. For the All-Ireland they resisted the temptation of availing of the customary six 'outside' players and decided to contest the game with hurlers from their own club only. They were hosted at a function in the North Star Hotel by the Dublin Wexfordmen's Association prior to the game. One of those in attendance at the function was Michael Cusack, one of the founding fathers of the Association, who was then very much out of favour with GAA officialdom.

5

1900s & '10s

LONDON JOINS THE CHAMPIONSHIP

It was the turn of a third townsland in the parish of Moycarkey to win the 1900 All-Ireland. Two-Mile-Borris represented Tipperary in the All-Ireland against the English champions, London Desmonds, the first year an English club played in the championship, and defeated them by 2-5 to 0-6 at Jones's Road on 26 October 1902. About 8,000 spectators turned up for the contest, which was described by *Sport* as 'the best, the cleverest and the fastest we have seen in an All-Ireland final.' Tipperary led by 5 points to 3 at the interval. In the second half London added 3 more points and were leading with three minutes remaining. Then luck favoured Tipperary. They got a free from which they scored a goal and, following the puck out, they rushed a second goal, to win by 2-5 to 0-6. Ned Hayes captained the winning side and the team included a number of Tubberadora and Horse & Jockey All-Ireland players.

LONDON'S ONE AND ONLY

When one looks at the Roll of Honour of All-Ireland winners, London stands out as the only team from outside the country to win the highest honour in hurling. The year was 1901, the venue was Jones's Road and the result was London Emmets 1-5 Cork (Redmonds) 0-4.

Cork were, without doubt, favourites to win the game but London had proved against Two-Mile-Borris the previous year that they could hurl. Cork probably took the game too casually and had little sleep the night before. The wet ground helped the well-equipped Emmets team and, despite the fact that Cork were the better hurlers, they had to concede victory to a powerful exiles' seventeen after a great game. A special train from Cork, carrying supporters to the game, was delayed by a troop train and arrived late in Dublin, where they heard the bad news that the final was over and Cork were beaten! The winners' seventeen included nine players from Cork, four from Clare, two from Limerick and one each from Tipperary and Kerry. This was London's finest hour and the only time the senior championship crossed the water. J.J. Coughlan (Tulla, Clare) captained the London Emmets side. The president of the London county board was William McCarthy, later to present the cup for the All-Ireland championship. Ned Barrett from Ballyduff, County Kerry, who was a policeman in London, had the added distinction of winning an Olympic gold medal for tug-a-war and a bronze medal for free-style wrestling in the 1908 games.

THE REBELS STRIKE BACK

Cork got their own back on London when they defeated them in the 1902 and 1903 finals. In fact, in the wake of the heavy defeats suffered by London in the finals, the Central Council decided to scrap the system of allowing the UK representatives (London up to that year) play the winners of the 'Home' final in the All-Ireland final. Subsequently the exiles were allowed into the championship at an earlier stage.

Cork (Dungourney) defeated London (Brian Boru) by 3-13 to 0-0 in the 1902 final, played at the new Athletic Grounds in Cork, before thousands of spectators on 11 September 1904.

In the 'Home' final Cork and Dublin (a Faughs/Commercials selection) drew 1-7 each at Tipperary on 3 July 1904. In the replay at the same venue two weeks later, Dublin were overwhelmed by 2-6 to 0-1. It was a tough confrontation and the proximity of spectators to the pitch encouraged many incursions on to the field. Some spectators had to be forcibly removed by the police and a number of people were arrested.

Cork (Blackrock) defeated London Irish by 3-16 to 1-1 at Jones's Road on 12 November 1905 in the 1903 final.

In the 'Home' final, played at Dungarvan on 15 July 1905, Cork (Blackrock) defeated Kilkenny (Three Castles) by 8-9 to 0-8. Andy Buckley of Cork was credited with scoring 6 goals. Little did anyone think after the 25 point drubbing that Kilkenny would be All-Ireland champions the following year!

HURLING GREATS

Outstanding Captain, Jim Kelliher (Cork) 1878-1943
Jim Kelliher of Dungourney, who captained the Cork team to All-Ireland honours in 1902, usually played at full-back but he was versatile enough to feature in other parts of the field as well. He wasn't a big man, 5 foot 9 inches in height, but was always fit and had a good temperament. He played for Cork from 1901 to 1912, winning two All-Irelands, 1902 and 1903, but losing four, 1904, 1905, 1907 and 1912 to Kilkenny. He also won seven Munster medals.

Jim Kelliher put Dungourney, which is situated in east Cork, on the map as a result of his outstanding hurling. Carbery, the great commentator on the game, had this to say about him: 'Kelliher had brains, skill, stamina and ash craft in abundance. I saw him play in twenty-six major matches and he never left the field without being the outstanding hurler of the hour.' He placed him centreback in his team entitled 'The Best Team of My Time'.

THE 'CATS' ARRIVE IN STYLE

The failure of Kilkenny to make an impact in hurling during the first twenty years of the GAA is difficult to comprehend in current times, when they are so much the dominant team that the All-Ireland could as well be fought-out between the county and the rest of the country.

Kilkenny was a different world at the end of the nineteenth century when cricket was king. The game had caught on and spread throughout the county and through the classes during the second half of the nineteenth century. Players included farm labourers and estate workers as well as the landed gentry. It reached its peak in 1896 when there were over fifty teams of eleven in the county.

When the GAA was founded in 1884 the games of hurling and football were slow to take off and of the two, football was much the stronger. For instance, in the 1889 long kick championship of Ireland, Matty Downey of Conahy, Ballyragget beat the legendary J.P. O'Sullivan of Laune Rangers, Killorglin. In 1887 Michael Cusack's *Sport* noted that the game of hurling in the city of Kilkenny drew no spectators, proving 'what little hold the GAA has taken on Kilkenny.' Worse than the lack of spectators, however, was the quality of play: 'The hurling of both teams was, we believe, the worst and most spiritless ever witnessed on an Irish hillside,' he lamented. 'It would break the heart of a Moycarkey or Galway Gael to witness such a contemptible perversion of the grand old dashing game.'

Right up to 1903 hurling was poor as the 25 point drubbing of Kilkenny's Three Castles by Cork's Blackrock in the 1903 All-Ireland 'Home' final was undoubted testimony. And then as suddenly as a Damascine conversion, Kilkenny hurling was transformed.

SEVEN TITLES IN TEN YEARS, 1904-1913

When Kilkenny set out for Mountrath on 4 March 1906 to play Laois in the delayed Leinster championship of 1904, they began a campaign that culminated in their first All-Ireland victory. They went on to capture the title seven times in the next ten years (eight in fact, since the 1913 final was played in the calendar year) and established Kilkenny as one of the great hurling counties.

During these ten years four players figured on all seven winning teams. They were Sim Walton (Tullaroan), Jack Rochford (Threecastles), Dick Doyle and 'Drug' Walsh (Mooncoin).

HURLING GREATS

A Distinguished Captain, Tom Semple (Tipperary) 1879-1943
Thurles went through a lean hurling period after winning the first All-Ireland final and didn't get back into contention for hurling honours until 1904. The man responsible for their change in fortunes was Drombane native and captain, Tom Semple. He was a leader in the real sense of the word and insisted on nothing but the highest standards. He used innovative tactics and training methods. The team favoured a ground hurling style. Jack Mockler recounts how training under Semple involved the players lining up outside the Confraternity Hall, marching out to the Ragg, back in again to spend an hour or two skipping, some work on the punch ball and then a practice match!

Semple was handy with the ball in the hand also. He won the 1906 All-Ireland long puck championship, hitting the 9 ounce sliotar a distance of 96 yards. Semple, who was born in 1879, retired from inter-county hurling after defeat in the 1909 All-Ireland but continued playing for the Blues until 1912. His record included six county championships, four Munster titles (his first Munster and All-Ireland titles were won with Two-Mile-Borris in 1900), and three All-Irelands. The Munster win in 1909 was followed by defeat to Kilkenny in the All-Ireland.

In recognition of his exploits on the hurling field and his contribution to the GAA as an administrator at all levels from club through to national level, Thurles Sportsfield was renamed Semple Stadium in his honour in 1971.

THE STATISTICS

1904 Carrick-on-Suir (24 June 1906) Kilkenny (Tullaroan) 1-9 Cork
(St Finbarr's) 1-8

1905 Tipperary (14 April 1907) Cork (St Finbarr's) 5-10 Kilkenny
(Erin's Own) 3-13 (this was a disputed match and led to an
objection and counter-objection, then a replay)

Dungarvan (30 June 2007) Replay Kilkenny (Erin's Own) 7-7 Cork
(St Finbarr's) 2-9

1907 Dungarvan (21 June 1908) Kilkenny (Mooncoin) 3-12 Cork
(Dungourney) 4-8

1909 Cork (12 December 1909) Kilkenny (Mooncoin) 4-6 Tipperary
(Thurles) 0-12

1911 Cork (18 February 1912) Kilkenny (Tullaroan) declared
champions following a dispute with Limerick. In a substitute
contest, played at Dungarvan on 28 July 1912, Kilkenny beat
Tipperary (nominated by Munster Council) by 3-3 to 2-1

1912 Jones's Road (17 November 1912) Kilkenny (Tullaroan) 2-1
Cork (Blackrock) 1-3

1913 Croke Park (2 November 1913) Kilkenny (Mooncoin) 2-4
Tipperary (Toomevara) 1-2

THE STRIPY MEN

Prior to the 1911 final Kilkenny lined out in the colours of the county
champions. In that year John F. Drennan of Conway Hall in the parish
of Danesfort presented a set of black and amber jerseys to the Kilkenny
county board to be worn by the county team. The story is that the
colours were worn by a winning horse and the owner insisted, when the
winnings were being handed over to the Kilkenny county board, that
the county team play in the colours. The 1911 team couldn't use the
jerseys in the final because the game never took place owing to a dispute
about the venue. Kilkenny were declared champions and since then the
distinctive colours have been worn by the county. Kilkenny had lined
out in black and amber jerseys for the 1905 final and this was their first

time to win an All-Ireland in the famous colours. When Danesfort club was formed in 1922 they adopted the black and amber as their colours.

DISPUTE (1) A BRITISH ARMY RESERVIST IN GOALS!

Kilkenny (Erin's Own) played Cork (St Finbarr'a) in the 1905 final at Tipperary on 14 April 1907 and were beaten 5-10 to 3-13. Kilkenny objected to the victory on the grounds that Daniel McCarthy, the Cork goalkeeper, was illegal because he was a reservist in the British Army.

At the subsequent Central Council meeting, Cork raised a counter-objection to Matt Gargan of Kilkenny, claiming that he had played with Waterford in the Munster championship. A replay was proposed and agreed to on a 4-3 vote.

The replay was held at Dungarvan on 30 June 1907 before an estimated 10,000 spectators. Cork led by 2-6 to 2-2 at the interval. Kilkenny dominated the second-half and confined Cork to 3 points. Jim Kelly ran riot and is credited with scoring 5-2. The winning captain was Dan Stapleton (Erin's Own).

DISPUTE (2) A BOGGY PITCH

The 1911 final between Kilkenny (Tullaroan) and Limerick (Ballingarry) didn't take place because of a dispute about the venue. The match was fixed for Cork Athletic Grounds on 18 February 1912; however, heavy rain on the preceding days had left the pitch in a poor condition. When the Kilkenny officials arrived to inspect the ground they found the caretaker with his trousers tucked above his knees, attempting to mark the field. In dramatic circumstances Limerick had snatched victory from the jaws of defeat over Tipperary in similar conditions in the Munster final the previous November and wanted to play. In fact, the team had togged out and were pucking the ball around to the cheers of their supporters in the crowd of almost 14,000 spectators. However, the referee, Tom Kenny of Galway, along with some Central Council officials, inspected the pitch and declared it unplayable.

Central Council refixed the game for Thurles on 12 May 1912. Limerick refused to play at the new venue and declared for 'Cork or nowhere'. They appealed the matter to All-Ireland Congress, who confirmed Thurles as the venue by fifty-three votes to seventeen. Despite this, Limerick still persisted in their refusal and the Central Council, at a meeting held on 2 June, awarded the game and title to Kilkenny. Limerick county board were subsequently suspended for their failure to field a team on the occasion.

In order to compensate for the loss of revenue resulting from the lack of a fixture, the Central Council organised a game between Kilkenny and Tipperary, who were nominated by Munster Council as runners-up in the Munster championship, in lieu of the All-Ireland final. This was played at Dungarvan on 28 July 1912 for a special set of medals, valued at £20, which was a princely sum in those days. Following a hard-fought tie Kilkenny won by 3-3 to 2-1.

TOO GOOD FOR THE GREYHOUNDS

Kilkenny completed their great run of seven All-Ireland titles between 1904 and 1913 by winning their first three-in-a-row. In the third of these victories, the 1913 All-Ireland, they defeated the Tipperary champions, Toomevara.

Popularly known as the 'Greyhounds', because of their speed and fitness, and led by their inspirational captain, Widger Meagher, Tipperary went into this final as favourites. This status was mainly due to their defeat of Kilkenny in the Croke Memorial Tournament final by 5-4 to 1-4. The speed of this outfit had captured the hurling public's imagination and it was felt it would be too good for and ageing Kilkenny side. However, Kilkenny had been forewarned and put in two weeks of special training.

Tipperary's preparation for the final was upset by a dispute between the county board and the Central Council concerning the Dr Croke Memorial. The county board asked Toomevara not to play the final and they decided initially not to travel, but later reversed the decision.

A crowd of 12,000 attended the final and from their first score Kilkenny showed superiority. They had no problem matching Tipperary in the pace of the game. Kilkenny led by 1-4 to 1-1 at the interval and survived a Tipperary rally in heavy rain in the second-half to win by 2-4 to 1-2.

The defeat was a big disappointment for Toomevara, who had arrived on the scene as county champions in 1912 with great fanfare. They made it three-in-a-row in 1914, but were then beaten by great rivals, Boherlahan, over the next three years. They beat the mid men in 1918 but lost the match on an objection. They were to win four more county finals in 1919, 1923, 1930 and 1931 before disappearing from the scene for almost thirty years. They had to suffer the disappointment of never captaining the county to an All-Ireland victory during these years so maybe the defeat to Kilkenny in 1913 left longer lasting scars than was realised at the time.

THE THURLES BLUES

Thurles made history in 1888, when they won the first All-Ireland hurling championship in their original colours of green and gold. The club didn't hit the headlines again until 1904, when they won their second county championship under the inspirational leadership of their great captain, Tom Semple. By this stage they had changed their colours to blue and white and were known as the Thurles Blues.

Semple was the focal point of the team and his influence can't be emphasised enough. In eight years he led Thurles to six county titles, three Munster and two All-Ireland titles. Their All-Ireland titles interspersed the seven won by Kilkenny during the years 1904-1913. But Thurles didn't meet Kilkenny in either of them. In the 1906 final they defeated Dublin (Faughs) by 3-16 to 3-8 at Kilkenny on 27 October 1907. In the 1908 final they defeated Dublin (Kickhams) by 3-15 to 1-5 in a replay at Athy on 27 June 1909. When the sides met at Jones's Road on 25 April 1909 the game ended in a draw, Tipperary 2-5 Dublin 1-8.

The Blues did meet Kilkenny (Mooncoin) in the 1909 final but were defeated by 4-6 to 0-12 at Cork on 12 December 1909. Having beaten Dungourney in a dramatic late rally in the Munster final, the Blues were hopeful in their meeting with Mooncoin but their plans became unstuck in a near waterlogged pitch, which didn't suit the Blues ground hurling style. It was Tipperary's first defeat in a final.

The Blues won their last county final in 1912 and this was the end of the road for the famous team. They entered a lean period after that, squeezed out of honours by Toomevara and Boherlahan, and didn't return again to glory until 1929, seventeen years in the hurling wilderness, the same length of time they were there after the first All-Ireland.

FIFTH TIME LUCKY

It took Wexford five attempts before winning their first All-Ireland. They lost to Cork (Aughabullogue) in 1890, to Kerry (Ballyduff) in 1891, to Tipperary (Horse & Jockey) in 1899 and the 1901 'Home' final to Cork (Redmonds), before finally making the breakthrough against Limerick in 1910. Wexford (Castlebridge) defeated Limerick (Castleconnell) by 7-0 to 6-2 at Jones's Road on 20 November 1910.

It was the first day that sideline seats were in use at Jones's Road. Wexford led at the interval by 6-0 to 3-1 and seemed home and dry when they scored their seventh goal within minutes of the re-start. But Limerick were far from finished and reduced the margin to a single point before the final whistle.

Limerick had a goal disallowed near the end, which they claimed was unfair. They objected to the result but, because the objection wasn't lodged in duplicate, according to rule, the Central Council at its meeting on 4 December, refused to entertain it. Tyler Mackey was the Limerick captain.

One of the memorable things about the final was that it gave Wexford's Sean Kennedy and Paddy Mackey All-Ireland hurling medals prior to their four-in-a-row victories with the footballers.

HURLING GREATS

A Very Special Captain, Patrick 'Wedger' Meagher (Tipperary) 1890-1958

Patrick 'Wedger' Meagher is probably one of the greatest captains who never won an All-Ireland.

Born in Toomevara, he put the Tipperary parish on the map among Irishmen all over the world because of its association with him and the eponymous Greyhounds.

He was involved with horses from an early age and following a success at the local races, in which he made a very strong finish, he was nicknamed 'Widger', transmuted to 'Wedger' through use, after a contemporary County Waterford family of that name noted for breeding and racing horses.

He was dedicated to hurling and became a formidable corner-back. He became involved with the re-organisation of the local club and so began the era of the legendary Greyhounds. They won their first county final in 1910, followed by three-in-a-row between 1912 and 1914, when Wedger captained the team.

It is said that it was his organising ability, enthusiasm and leadership which were mainly responsible for the success of the team in the early years. The Greyhounds were also stimulated by their battles with the Leahy-powered Boherlahan teams of that era for supremacy within the county.

The highlight of his hurling days was victory over Kilkenny at Dungarvan in the Croke Cup final of 1913. It provided the material for the club's national anthem, 'Hurrah for Toomevara'. In light of later events and the failure to win an All-Ireland, it was a bit premature.

While still playing, Wedger became involved in the National independence movement. He recruited, organised and trained the local Volunteers. He took part in ambushes and spent time in prisons in Belfast, Limerick and Wormwood Scrubs.

He was secretary of the north board from 1914 to 1920 and of the county board from 1922 to 1927. He travelled to the US with the Tipperary team in 1926 and returned there in the following year to spend the remainder of his life in New York. He became Sports Editor of the *Irish Echo* and his column, 'Games of the Gaels', became famous far and wide.

During the thirty-odd years he spent in New York, he made only a couple of visits home. He had married Ellen Whelehan, a near neighbour from Toomevara, in 1926, and the couple had two children. The best man at the wedding was his great friend and rival, Johnny Leahy of Boherlahan. Meagher died in 1958 and was buried far from his native place in the city of New York.

ONE FOR THE BANNER

Clare (Quin) defeated Laois (Kilcotton) by 5-1 to 1-0 in the 1914 final played at Croke Park on 18 October. It was the first appearance of a team from either county in the All-Ireland. A crowd of 12,127, including Willie Redmond, MP for East Clare, paid £475 to see the contest. Clare had trained under Jim Hehir of Ballynacally, father of the famous broadcaster, Micheal. The game was described as a 'tame struggle' in spite of expectations of a lively contest based on the fact that Laois had defeated three-in-a-row champions Kilkenny in the Leinster final. As it happened, Laois's efforts at close range left a lot to be desired and they lost by 'six scores to one' on a scoreline of 5-1 to 1-0, having been led by 3-1 to nil at the interval. Following the victory the Clare captain, Amby Power, who stood 6 foot 4 inches tall and was built accordingly, collected the Great Southern Challenge Cup, and the after-match celebrations took place in Wynne's Hotel. Clare had the added satisfaction of winning the junior hurling All-Ireland in the same year. This second hurling competition had been introduced for the first time in 1912.

According to one newspaper report, 'Several ladies with collecting boxes in aid of the rifle fund of the Irish Volunteers reaped a rich harvest from the crowd, a strong contrast to the cold reception given to the few ladies soliciting support for the Women's Suffrage cause.'

A LONE LAOIS VICTORY

Laois won their only All-Ireland senior hurling title in 1915 when the county, represented by Ballygeehan, defeated Cork (Redmonds) in the final played at Croke Park on October 24.

Laois were helped to prepare for the final by the legendary Dick 'Drug' Walsh of Mooncoin. He used his influence to bring the Kilkenny team to Portlaoise on three consecutive Sundays before the final to give Laois the practice they so badly needed.

Both teams travelled to Dublin on Saturday for the game. Laois wore black and amber hoops while Cork wore yellow jerseys. The teams took the field amidst a drenching downpour.

Among the 15,000 spectators at the game was a heavyweight boxing champion, Jack Johnston, then in revue at a Dublin music hall. He appeared to be a supporter of Laois too!

Laois had many wides in the first twenty minutes while Cork scored 2 goals. Laois began to play better after that and were behind by a point, 3-0 to 2-2, at the interval. They were on top in the second half and deserved their 6-2 to 4-1 victory.

Most of the winning side travelled home by train on Monday, alighting at Abbeyleix to a cordial reception. The captain, Jack Finlay, was borne shoulder high through the town while the town pipers' band and about seventy cars took part in the triumphal procession.

Jackie Carroll, who captained Kilcotton to defeat in the 1914 final and helped his county win the 1915 decider, was the last surviving member of these teams and died in September 1977, just six months short of his 100th birthday.

POLITICS AND SPORT

From the beginning the British Government believed that the GAA was a subversive organisation, dedicated to the overthrow of its rule in Ireland. They were convinced that the organisation set up in 1884 was really the creation of the Irish Republican Brotherhood.

While the aim of Michael Cusack and Maurice Davin at the Thurles meeting was to change how sport was organised in the country and give Gaelic games a proper place in the lives of Irish people, the GAA was always more than a sporting organisation.

From the beginning the organisation identified with nationalism and, because of the constituency to which it appealed, inevitably with Catholicism. No sooner was it in existence than it fell under the control of the IRB and that influence was to remain strong until after the Parnellite split.

Nationalist sentiment increased during the first decade of the twentieth century with the GAA tending to take the side of anti-British forces not only within the country but outside it as well. For instance the Kilruane club in County Tipperary changed its name to Lahorna de Wets in sympathy with the Boers. The ban on British forces and the Royal Irish Constabulary becoming members of the GAA was an expression of this sentiment.

The GAA supported the Irish Volunteers and there was a big overlap of GAA figures in the movement. Many joined the British Army at the beginning of the First World War. Following the failure to get Home Rule many members of the GAA drifted towards the new Irish Volunteers and it is estimated that about one-fifth of those who rose out in Easter Week were GAA members. The round-up of insurgents after the Rising included many members of the organisation.

The GAA identified with Sinn Féin after the Rising and held tournaments to raise funds for republican prisoners. The British Government singled out the GAA as part of the enemy and insisted on the organisation having permits to hold matches. The GAA were involved in the emergence of the Irish Republican Army.

Bloody Sunday in November 1920 was an indication of how the British regarded the GAA as a threat and, on the other hand, the impact of the event was to be huge on the national consciousness and confirmed the organisation as one of the foremost nationalistic bodies in the country.

Like the country itself the GAA were split by the Civil War but because the divided members remained in contact through the playing of games, the organisation provided a common ground for the eventual easing of the bitterness of the civil strife.

BOHERLAHAN AND
THE YEAR OF THE RISING

It was fitting that Tipperary, represented by Boherlahan, a place where national sentiment was strong, should win the 1916 All-Ireland, the year of the Rising. The parish was the home of the small townsland of Tubberadora as well as Suir View and Ballytarsna, who also had teams of note. The new club was formed in 1912 but had to play second fiddle to Toomevara until 1915. Beaten by Cork that year in Munster, they went all the way to the All-Ireland in 1916, which wasn't played until January 1917, and defeated Kilkenny (Tullaroan) by 5-4 to 3-2.

The game took place in the atmosphere of tension and imprisonments that followed the Rising. Tipperary led by 1-2 to 0-1 at the break but Kilkenny came out a transformed team in the second half and were 2 points in front with ten minutes remaining. At this stage Dick Grace of Kilkenny and Tommy Shanahan of Tipperary were sent off, and the Kilkenny loss was much the greater. Tipperary rallied and in a tremendous finish snatched victory from the jaws of defeat.

Denis Walsh won his fifth All-Ireland medal on the day, twenty-one years after winning his first with Tubberadora in 1895. Having won three with Tubberadora, he helped Horse & Jockey to theirs in 1899 after which he retired. In 1912 he was one of the movers in the foundation of Boherlahan and came out of retirement to win three county finals and his fifth All-Ireland in 1916.

Boherlahan had a 50 per cent record during these years. Later the same year they were defeated by Dublin (Collegians) in the 1917 All-Ireland by 5-4 to 4-2, probably through over-confidence. Johnny Leahy said later: 'We thought we were going to wallop the schoolboys but 'twas they taught us our lessons.' Dublin, on the other hand, were well prepared. They brought a new dimension to training; 'track gallops, baths, massage and handball took the place of older methods.'

TOSSED HIS HURLEY AND BOOTS INTO THE LIFFEY

Tipperary lost again in 1922 when Kilkenny snatched victory from the jaws of defeat. With ten minutes remaining they were 7 points in arrears but, in the briefest time, they flashed 2 goals into the Tipperary net, and then another to take the lead. Tipperary retaliated with a point but Kilkenny got the final score to win by 4-2 to 2-6. It was to be Kilkenny's last victory over Tipperary in a major hurling competition until 1967. Jack Cleary of Toomevara, a clerical student at the time, who played centrefield for Tipperary on the day, was so disgusted with the defeat that he tossed his hurley and boots into the Liffey as he walked to Kingsbridge Station for the train home.

Boherlahan won their second All-Ireland in 1926 when they beat Galway by 5-6 to 1-5 in the final.

There were two innovations in Croke Park for the final. A scoreboard was erected on the railway wall and the Artane Boys Band gave a display of gymnastics, as well as a selection of music. It was Tipperary's first time to receive the McCarthy Cup and the second time for Johnny Leahy to captain an All-Ireland side.

A FAMOUS HURLING FAMILY

The Leahys were synonymous with Boherlahan and Tipperary hurling. Captain Johnny, as he was known, who captained the county in the 1916 final and was to do so again in 1925, led Tipperary to five Munster championships, two All-Irelands and one National League title. He also led Tipperary on their American trip in 1926. Paddy also won All-Irelands in 1916 and 1925 and, as manager, was the chief architect of the county's dazzling success between 1949 and 1966. Mick won All-Irelands with Tipperary in 1916 and with Cork in 1928 and 1931, while the youngest, Tommy, won the highest honour in the game in 1930.

DUBLIN'S GREATEST ERA

Dublin's victory over Tipperary in the 1917 All-Ireland was to usher in the greatest era of hurling in Dublin. Over a period of eleven years the county was to dominate the All-Ireland championship, playing in six finals and winning four.

Dublin had lost six finals prior to the 1917 victory and had been strengthened by the influx of players from the country, who had taken up employment in the city and had to declare for Dublin because of the residence rule.

They lost the 1919 final to Cork, who won their first final in fifteen years, but avenged the defeat the following year. Dublin (Faughs) had ten players on the team, including Bob Mockler, who played in seven All-Irelands, and Jim 'Builder' Walsh, a native of Mooncoin, who played with Kilkenny between 1915 and 1919 before moving to Dublin and joining Faughs. He played with them for fifteen years, winning six county championships and three All-Irelands. Also included was Jim Cleary of Kilruane, who joined them as a sixteen-year-old in 1907 and won his eighth county championship medal in 1923. Dublin won by 4-9 to 4-3.

Dublin lost heavily to Limerick in the 1921 final but succeeded against favourites, Galway, by 5-3 to 2-6 in 1924.

With the setting up of the Free State and the formation of the new army and Garda, the flow of players to Dublin increased. This added strength was shown in their victory over a strong Cork team in the 1927 final. In the Leinster final it was Dublin's Kilkennymen, Jim 'Builder' Walsh and Mattie Power, who were the stars of a 7-7 to 4-6 victory. In the All-Ireland Cork were 'outpaced and outplayed by probably the best fifteen who have ever contested a championship final' and Dublin won by 4-8 to 1-3. Two Claremen, who were to be on the losing side to Kilkenny in the 1932 All-Ireland, contributed significantly to the victory. Dr Tommy Daly was outstanding in goals and Fowler

HURLING GREATS

Little Sim Walton (Kilkenny) 1880-1966

Simon Walton (Tullaroan), better known as Sim and familiarly as Little Sim, was born in 1880 and died in 1966.

He is synonymous with the great Kilkenny period of success between 1904 and 1913 when he was one of four players to win all seven All-Irelands. He was captain on two occasions, in 1911, when no final was played because Limerick refused to agree to a change of venue, and 1912, when he scored the winning goal against Cork in the final.

He was also captain in 1916 when Kilkenny were beaten by Tipperary in the final. Not a big man, Sim weighed about eleven stone and was of average height. He was noted for his sudden bursts of speed and his accuracy and these attributes, plus his outstanding skill, made him a notable forward who could play effectively in the centre or full positions.

His inter-county career spanned the years 1903 to 1919. He won ten Leinster titles and seven county championships with Tullaroan. He was a legendary character and his name evokes greatness and outstanding ability.

(the nickname was attributed to ancestors who were adept at shooting wild fowl on the East Clare lake margins) McInerney at full-back gave him great protection. The strength of the team was recognised with the selection of nine players on the Leinster team.

The sides were to meet again in the 1928 All-Ireland semi-final, which was arranged for the official opening of Nowlan Park on 28 August, when the result was reversed in emphatic fashion. Part of the reason was the passing of the Declaration Rule, which came into operation that year. Under this rule a player living away could declare for his native county. This was to greatly deplete Dublin as a hurling force and they were to win only one more All-Ireland, in 1938.

6

1920s & '30s

THE LIAM MCCARTHY CUP

The Liam McCarthy Cup, indelibly associated with the All-Ireland senior hurling championship, was first presented to the winners, Limerick, after the 1921 final, which wasn't played until 4 March 1923 because of the unsettled state of the country.

It was announced at the GAA Congress that William McCarthy, who was active in the London GAA and in national circles, intended to present a cup for the All-Ireland hurling championship. Apparently McCarthy, who was born in London of Irish parents in 1853, had invested £50 to purchase ten certificates in the Irish loan scheme set up by Michael Collins. As the money was now being redeemed he sought a further means of supporting a worthy cause. His friend, Dan Fraher of Dungarvan, suggested that it be used for an All-Ireland trophy. The new trophy, which was made by Edmund Johnson, Jewellers of Grafton Street, Dublin, and which cost £50, was presented by the president of the GAA, Dan McCarthy, to the Limerick captain, Bob McConkey, amid scenes of great excitement.

Limerick defeated Dublin by 8-5 to 3-2 in a very disappointing final before 20,000 spectators, who paid £1,680 to see the game. James O'Mara, of the O'Mara Opera Company, a native of Limerick, threw in the ball for the start of the final.

PREVIOUS ALL-IRELAND TROPHIES

Prior to the presentation of the McCarthy Cup, not every winner of the All-Ireland championship was presented with a trophy. On the occasion of his Episcopal Silver Jubilee in July 1896, Archbishop Thomas Croke, presented two silver cups to the GAA. One of the cups was presented for a secondary hurling competition, which was won by Clare in the inaugural year. Limerick won it in 1897.

Because of the difficulty of running off the competition in time, the GAA decided in 1898 to present the Croke Cup to the All-Ireland champions. Tubberadora, as All-Ireland champions, were presented with the Croke Cup in 1898 and this arrangement continued until 1901.

There was a new arrangement in 1902 and 1903, when the Croke Cup was presented to the winners of a competition between the provinces. The cup was not awarded in 1904 and 1905. In the years 1906 and 1908 it was awarded to the Croke Cup competition winners. From 1909 to 1915 the Croke Cup was awarded to the winners of a new competition between the four beaten provincial finalists. In 1916 this competition was dropped and the cup was retired.

In 1926 the Croke Cup was taken out of retirement and presented to the winners of the National League. It continued to be presented until 2006, when it was placed in the GAA Museum in Croke Park.

From 1901 until 1912 no trophy was presented to the All-Ireland winners. In 1913, the Great Southern and Western Railway Company presented a cup to the GAA for the All-Ireland hurling champions. This cup was to become the 'absolute property' of the first county to win the All-Ireland title twice in succession. No county won the All-Ireland title twice during the years 1913 to 1920. The winners during the period were Kilkenny, Clare, Laois, Tipperary, Dublin, Limerick, Cork and Dublin. When Dublin won the cup in 1920, they were represented by Faughs and the cup now stands in their clubhouse in Templeogue.

Between 1887 and 1920 the All-Ireland winners of the years 1898 and 1901, and the years 1913 and 1920 were presented with a trophy. The winners in the other years were not.

GALWAY WIN THEIR FIRST ALL-IRELAND

After thirty-six years of endeavour Galway won their first All-Ireland in 1923. They had appeared in the first All-Ireland and contested the 'Home' final in 1900 but that was the end of their achievement. They reached the 1923 final in style, beating reigning All-Ireland champions Kilkenny in the semi-final. The final, against Limerick, was played at Croke Park on 24 September 1924. One of the players, Jim Power of Tynagh, recalled the preparations in an interview at the age of 100 in 1995. The team had organised collective training in order to improve their chances:

> We stayed in this place between Athenry and Craughwell, a lovely place. There was a big gentleman's place on the estate, a big, vast house, and there was every accommodation for the team to train. There were grand fields and a lovely ball alley. For nearly three weeks we trained there.

Jim was full-back, in his seventh season on the team and at the height of his powers. In those days full-back was a thorny place:

> It was the awfulest place on the field: all the tough going was there. The only thing for it was first-time pulling. When I trained I had a man thirty yards away from me and he banged in balls, left and right, overhead, this side, that side. I never tried to stop that ball or catch it. I was all the time pulling first time. In the end very few balls passed me.

Galway qualified for the 1924 All-Ireland, which was played three months after they had won the 1923 final. They had virtually the same team. They played reasonably well in the first half against Dublin, and led at half-time, but they failed to raise a flag in the second half and were beaten by 5-3 to 2-6. So, in the space of three months they had won and lost an All-Ireland.

Galway played in their third-in-a-row final in 1925 and came up against Tipperary, whom they had beaten in the previous year's semi-final. On this occasion they were outclassed by their opponents and beaten by 5-6 to 1-5. Galway weren't to make a hurling impact again until the late 1940s.

HURLING GREATS

Mick Gill – Two All-Irelands in One Year –
(Galway and Dublin) 1899-1980

Mick Gill of Ballinderreen, County Galway, had the distinction of winning two All-Irelands in the space of three months with two counties. He played his early hurling with his native club and came to prominence with the county team in 1922. His big moment came in 1923 when Galway defeated Limerick in the All-Ireland final, which wasn't played until 14 September 1924. (Limerick refused to play this final until all Civil War prisoners were released and were initially disqualified but were later reprieved.) Galway won by 7-3 to 4-5 in a game in which Gill made a major contribution at midfield with his ploy of lobbing the ball into the square.

In 1924 Gill joined the new Garda force and as such went to live in Dublin, where he joined the Garda club. He was thus qualified to play with Dublin in the 1924 championship and he was on the team that won the Leinster final and defeated Antrim in the All-Ireland semi-final. He came up against his native county in the All-Ireland, which was played on 14 December, just three months after winning the 1923 final, and he won his second All-Ireland when Dublin won by 5-3 to 2-6.

He won his second Leinster medal and his third All-Ireland captaining Dublin, when they defeated Cork in the 1927 final. He won two further Leinster medals in 1928 and 1930. He returned to the Galway colours in 1931 and continued to play with them until 1938, when he retired after sixteen years of inter-county hurling.

Gill also lined out in the inter-provincial competition with his adopted province of Leinster. He won his sole Railway Cup medal in 1927, the inaugural year of the competition. He was on the Ireland hurling team in the 1928 Tailteann Games. He won a National Hurling League title in 1929. He enjoyed much success with the Garda club in the Dublin championship, winning six county titles between 1925 and 1931.

Mick Gill, whose best playing position was right wind-back, died on 21 September 1980, one day short of his 81st birthday and just two weeks after the Galway hurlers bridged a fifty-seven-year gap to capture their second All-Ireland title.

TRIP TO THE USA

Following victory in the 1925 All-Ireland, the Tipperary county board were issued with an invitation to travel to the US by Paddy Cahill, a prominent barrister in Chicago and a native of Holycross. The object in view was the popularising of the Irish games in the USA, the testing of the exiles' prowess in the national pastime of hurling, and the hope of making the annual hurling championship an international event, at least as far as American was concerned. A party of twenty-five players and officials travelled to America in May 1926 on an eleven-week tour, during which they played six games, two in New York, one at each end of the tour, and one each in Boston, San Francisco, Buffalo and Chicago. They were victorious in all and attendances were big, with 30,000 in New York and 15,000 in San Francisco.

One of the players was Tom Duffy and, in an interview in 1981, he stated that he didn't remember much about the games but recalled prohibition and the speakeasies. He remembered fun and games with Jim O'Meara on Coney Island and a mystery tunnel tour with Stephen Kenny. 'We nearly died from the heat. I remember us sitting on the verandas with our mouths open panting like dogs. 'Twas too hot to put our coats on our shoulders.'

Another member of the party, Tom Kenny, wrote an account of the tour and Tom Duffy features more often in it than any other member of the party. There are about twenty references to him; he was the life and the soul of the party. The entry for 7 June reads: 'Tom Duffy is singing that song "The next I met was a fair-haired lady, standing at a cottage door".' And on 9 June there is a discussion between Jack Power and Tom on the state of the country: 'A crock of a country', says Duffy. 'Sure we haven't seen a tram of hay, a ditch, nor a hedge since leaving the old country, but it is a fine country in other ways, Jack – they do everything the big way.' Duffy thinks the Yanks made a mistake to set the country dry. 'That hooch is rotten stuff, Jack, and if it continues as plentiful as it seems to be it will make mad men, blind men or dead men of all of them that drink it.' On 19 June there is a party on the train and Duffy dances a jig. Later Paddy Leahy and Tom try to sing the last verse of the Star-Spangled Banner at the Eucharistic Congress in Chicago. Later still we learn that five hurlers are found in Duffy's Chicago hotel room saying the rosary. On the ship home he is constantly playing his favourite deck game and won 'Chalking the Pig's Eye' in the ship's sports. Truly a man of many sides!

A GREAT CORK ERA

Cork dominated the period 1926 to 1931, during which they won four All-Irelands and two National Leagues. The era was ushered in with three exciting games against Tipperary in 1926 and climaxed by three thrilling encounters with Kilkenny five years later.

In the three games against Tipperary in the 1926 Munster championship, the first game at the Athletic Grounds had to be abandoned because of crowd encroachment. The re-fixed game at Thurles before 27,000 spectators ended in a draw and the replay at the same venue attracted a new record crowd of 30,000. Cork's greater youth and exuberance won out in the end, aided by the fact that Tipperary's Martin Mockler was sent off ten minutes into the game. Cork went on to defeat Kilkenny in the All-Ireland final. Cork also won the National League.

Cork were shocked in the 1927 final when they were outplayed and outpaced by Dublin, who won by 4-8 to 1-3. The defeat turned out to be only a temporary blip as they annihilated all opposition in the 1928 championship before destroying Galway by 6-12 to 1-0 in the All-Ireland final.

Cork defeated Galway, who had a great victory over Kilkenny in the semi-final, once again in the 1929 final. Galway tried to motivate its players in the game by having their hurleys inscribed with the words: *Remember Mick King*, a reference to their best forward, who had his leg broken in the 1928 All-Ireland, but it was to no avail and they were beaten by 4-9 to 1-3.

Cork were surprisingly knocked out of the Munster championship by Clare in 1930 but had the consolation of winning their second National League. Tipperary won the All-Ireland.

Cork came back in the 1931 championship, beating Clare, Tipperary, and Waterford in a replayed Munster final to qualify for the All-Ireland final against Kilkenny on the first Sunday in September. This was a rousing encounter, which ended in a draw when Cork's Eudie Coughlan struck the ball over the bar for the equalising point, while he was down on his knees! The replay five weeks later was a superb game and voted the greatest hurling exhibition of all time. Cork led by 2-4 to 1-3 at the interval and their only score in the second-half was an equalising point, as the sides finished 2-5 each. Even greater interest was generated by the second replay, which didn't take place until November. A proposal to have the teams declared joint champions was defeated at Central Council by ten votes to six. The lateness of the year reduced the crowd somewhat and Kilkenny were without their star performer, Lory Meagher. Cork got 2 goals just before half-time to lead by 2-5 to 1-2. In the second-half Kilkenny came storming back and came within a point of Cork amid tremendous excitement. But, as if the effort were too great for them, Cork pulled away again to win easily by 5-8 to 3-4.

HURLING GREATS

Dinny Barry Murphy (Cork) 1904-1973

One of the outstanding hurlers on the Cork team at this time was Dinny Barry Murphy, who was born in Cloughduf in 1904 and initially played junior hurling with them and won an All-Ireland junior title with Cork in 1925. He played senior with Blackrock in 1927 and won a county title. The following year Cloughduf and Bride Rovers combined to form Eire Óg and won the county championship. Murphy played with Eire Óg until 1932, when he transferred to St Finbarr's and played with them until 1936. He resumed with Cloughduf in 1937 and won county junior and intermediate title in successive years, 1940 and 1941. He played senior hurling once again in the 1942 championship, his last playing season.

Lightly built, Dinny Barry Murphy played at right wing-back and was regarded as one of the greatest hurlers of all time. A piece of doggerel from the period captures something of the man:

> Dinny Barry Murphy, boy,
> Great hurler, boy!
> He'd take the ball out of your eye, boy,
> And he wouldn't hurt a fly, boy!

He played senior hurling for Cork from 1926 to 1935, during which time he won four All-Ireland titles including in 1929 when he was captain. He won National League titles in 1926 and 1930. Playing in the inaugural Railway Cup provincial championship in 1927 was the first of eight successive appearance he made for Munster, winning five, including 1930 as captain. He was a sub on the successful 1935 team and won his sixth medal. He represented Ireland in the 1932 Tailteann Games.

Eudie Coughlan, whose contribution to Cork's victory on the day was enormous, later stated: 'Kilkenny were a young team coming along that year. We were old and experienced, nearing the end of our tether, if you like. I think that was one of the main reasons that Cork won.' How right he was! During the next decade Kilkenny went on to win four All-Irelands, while Cork's name wouldn't appear even once on the roll of champions.

INCREASED POPULARITY OF THE GAME

The three-game saga, between Cork and Tipperary in 1926 and Cork and Kilkenny in 1931, generated great publicity for the game of hurling. Two developments facilitated this. The second match against Tipperary was one of the first matches to be broadcast on radio and the voice of P.D. Mehigan ('Carbery') brought news of the game to many who weren't or couldn't be present. Increased coverage in local and national newspapers boosted popularity. The *Irish Press* first appeared on the eve of the 1931 All-Ireland and its sports editor, Joe Sherwood, realised that Irish people had a passion for sport which could be harnessed to sell his newspaper.

After the political turbulence of the 1920s relative political peace had arrived and the smooth political changeover from Cumann na nGaedheal to Fianna Fáil in the general election of 1932, confirmed this. With the arrival of peace, people could concentrate on more leisurely pursuits.

Another development about this time also increased the popularity of hurling. Two new competitions were introduced. The National League commenced in 1926 with twelve teams participating and it was a great success. The first final of the new provincial competition for the Railway Cup was played on St Patrick's Day 1927 and it turned out to be an outstanding encounter between the best players from Leinster and Munster. As the game reached its climax only a point, in favour of Leinster, stood between the teams, and it was Lory Meagher who scored the deciding one to give Leinster a 2-point victory on a scoreline of 1-11 to 2-6.

ALMOST CLARE'S YEAR

The year 1931 will live in Clare hurling memory as almost a great year. They didn't spring unheralded on the scene in that year but had been progressing over a number of years. In the inaugural National League in 1926 they won Division 2. They were beaten in the 1927, 1928 and 1930 Munster finals. They gave a superb performance in the 1931 final to defeat Cork by 5-2 to 4-1. In an extraordinary All-Ireland semi-final against Galway they came from 15 points down early in the second-half to score 7 goals and win by 9-4 to 4-14.

Galway were stunned by Clare's transformation and advanced three possible explanations:

A. the bottle that supplied mouthwash to the Clare players was dosed with poitín
B. the Munster champions changed the sliotar at half-time and played with a brilliant white ball in the second half
C. Biddy Early, the noted Clare witch of the late nineteenth century, had cast a spell over the Galway team

The 'spell' didn't last for the All-Ireland in which Kilkenny led by 2 points with a couple of minutes to go. At this stage Clare star, Tull Considine, was in possession near the Kilkenny goal. 'I steadied myself to make sure. There must be no mistake. I knew this was my last chance. And so I swung – but before my hurley had even connected with the ball, I was pushed in the back and thrown forward. It must be a twenty-one yard free, I thought, but we got no free.'

The Kilkenny version is different. 'With only two points between the sides, Clare made a last desperate effort and their star forward, Tull Considine, gained possession and got past Peter O'Reilly. It looked all over for Kilkenny. Then out of nowhere came Podge Byrne and his tackle put Considine off and his shot went wide. It was a save in a million and probably won the All-Ireland for Kilkenny.'

The Noresiders recovered and clinched the title with a point from Matty Power in the last minute for a final score of 3-3 to 2-3.

KILKENNY AND LIMERICK
VIE FOR SUPREMACY

The 1930s are remembered as the period of Limerick's greatest hurling era but, during the same period, Kilkenny wrote one of the finest chapters in the county's hurling history. A look at the record for the decade puts each county's achievements into perspective. During the ten years from 1931 to 1940 Kilkenny played in eight All-Irelands, winning four. After the three-game saga against Cork in 1931, they won three during the following four years and then lost two on the trot. They came back to win in 1939 and lose the following year. During the same period Limerick played in five All-Irelands, winning three. Two of these victories were over Kilkenny, as were two defeats. Because of the dominance of the two teams, there were meagre pickings for the other counties. Dublin qualified for two All-Irelands, losing in 1934 and winning in 1938. Cork won in 1931 but lost in 1939. Tipperary were successful in 1937, while Clare in 1932 and Waterford in 1938 fell at the final hurdle.

LIMERICK DOMINATE
THE NATIONAL LEAGUE

Limerick reigned supreme in the National League. In fact, the great Kilkenny-Limerick rivalry could be said to have started with the National League final of 1932-33, which the Noresiders won decisively by 3-8 to 1-3. Following this defeat Limerick were to record five consecutive victories, while Kilkenny had no further success.

Two of Limerick's victories were decided by a final. In the 1934 final Limerick defeated Dublin by 3-6 to 3-3 and they defeated Tipperary by 5-2 to 1-1 in the 1938 final. Between these years they won three leagues on point totals. In 1935 they won with 15 points from eight games. They had the same number of points in the 1936 league and they won the 1937 league with 13 points.

The crunch game for Limerick in the 1935 league was their game against Kilkenny at Nowlan Park, which they won by 1-6 to 1-4 in a highly competitive game. With the sides level near the end, Limerick won the spellbinding game with 2 late points from Mick Mackey and Mick Ryan. In the 1936 league the crunch game was also against Kilkenny and a great crowd attended in the hope of a classic. However, Limerick had a surprisingly easy victory by 6-1 to 1-2. Limerick ran riot against Cork in the final game of the 1937 league, winning by 11-6 to 5-1. Cork, with Jack Lynch as captain, conceded 4 goals in a devastating eight-minute spell in the first half and thereafter 'were swept aside in a tidal wave of green shirts.'

Limerick are the only county to win five National Hurling League titles in successive years. Four players participated in all five finals, Mick Kennedy (Young Ireland) captain, 1934; Timmy Ryan (Ahane) captain, 1935 and 1936; Mick Mackey (Ahane) captain, 1937 and 1938; Jim Roche (Croom).

A SPECIAL TRAIN TO THE MATCH

On their way to the 1933 All-Ireland, Limerick beat the reigning champions, Clare, in the first round at Thurles. An unusual feature of the game was the chartering of a special train to bring two players, Sergeant-Major Jim Houlihan of Clare, who was playing with Army Metro, and Christy O'Brien of Limerick, who was playing with Young Irelands, from Dublin, where they were playing an important championship game in the morning. It was realised that no car could do the journey to Thurles in the interval between the two games and it was arranged with the railway company to provide a fast non-stop train to Thurles. It was supposed to be the fastest engine in Ireland at the time. In good sporting fashion Christy O'Brien was given a lift on the train and both players arrived in time for the throw-in at Thurles.

The up-and-coming Limerick team won, went on to defeat Cork in the semi-final and were awarded the final game with Waterford at Cork, when the pitch was invaded eight minutes from the end. The All-Ireland final against Kilkenny attracted unprecedented interest because the sides had already met in the National League final. The attendance of 45,000 at Croke Park, with another 5,000 unable to gain admission, smashed all existing records for a sporting event in Ireland. The game lived up to expectations, played at a breathless pace, with the grimness and determination of both sides reflected in the half-time score of 0-4 each. The game continued close after the interval and remained so until a dazzling Johnny Dunne goal gave Kilkenny the edge and eventual victory by 1-7 to 0-6.

JUBILEE CHAMPIONS

Limerick won the 1934 final which was referred to as the Jubilee All-Ireland as the GAA celebrated fifty years in existence. Instead of meeting Kilkenny, their opponents were Dublin, who had beaten Kilkenny in a replayed Leinster final. Limerick had to overcome Clare, Cork, Waterford and Galway to reach the final. Limerick trained as never before for the final and came to Croke Park in peak condition. Dublin proved a formidable opposition and came from 5 points down, levelling the game with a last-minute goal. For the replay Limerick invited the Cork trainer, Jim Barry, to help them in their preparation. The sides were level at half-time and Dublin went into a three-point lead during the second half. However, great play by John Mackey turned the tide in Limerick's favour, and great goals by Dave Clohessy – four in all – ensured a Limerick victory by 5-2 to 2-6.

An elated Limerick captain, Timmy Ryan, received the cup from Dr Harty, the patron of the GAA. Never was a demonstration of such size seen in Limerick as the one that greeted the hurling heroes on their return to the city the following evening, when an estimated 30,000 people crowded the route from the railway station to the Imperial Hotel in Catherine Street.

VYING FOR SUPREMACY

The intensity of the rivalry between Kilkenny and Limerick during the 1930s can be gleaned from the newspaper coverage of the time. Following Kilkenny's victory by 2-5 to 2-4 in the 1935 final the following appeared in the report of the game in the *Kilkenny Post*:

> Kilkenny's hurling idols have carried the day. The very laws of nature have been defied. The veterans, the stale champions of 1933, have rocked the Gaelic world to its foundations with an amazing comeback, a glorious and memorable victory. Tradition has been upheld, nay, enriched a thousandfold and the children of Clann na nGaedhael worship at the shrine of Kilkenny – the nation's greatest hurlers.

In spite of the defeat, the Limerick hurlers were well-received in their city the following night. The players were carried shoulder-high to their hotel, and the mayor in his address assured them that their prestige was in no way diminished by the defeat.

HURLING GREATS

Mick Mackey (Limerick) 1912-1972
Mick Mackey, who was born in Castleconnell in 1912, was a colossus among hurlers and vies with Christy Ring and, perhaps, Henry Shefflin for the title of greatest hurler of all time. He starred during the golden age of Limerick hurling in the 1930s and his personal greatness made a major contribution to the golden age.

He played his hurling with Ahane and the club became famous all over Ireland for its exploits. During his playing years with the club, 1930 to 1948, he won fifteen county Limerick championships in hurling and five in football, and won many tournaments as well.

There was a great concentration of talent in Limerick at the time and it came to fruition in 1932. Mackey was the star of this team and his status as one of the all-time greats is unquestionable. In a senior inter-county career that lasted for seventeen years he was the pivotal player around whom success was achieved. He is regarded as the player who perfected the solo run and was reputed to carry the ball in his hand when he had his back to the referee!

During this period he won three All-Irelands and five Munster titles. He was also a member of five successive National League winning teams in 1933, 1934, 1935, 1936 and 1937. He won eight Railway Cup medals with Munster between 1934 and 1945. He won an Oireachtas medal in 1939, the inaugural year of the tournament, and eight Thomond Shield medals between 1932 and 1945. (Limerick also won in 1947 but it doesn't appear that Mackey was on the team.) Other achievements include an All-Army championship in 1943, two Limerick junior hurling and one Limerick minor hurling championships, and a Clare minor hurling championship.

Mackey was also part of the Limerick team's thirty-one-game unbeaten run between October 1933 and August 1935. This sequence of victories included eight championship, thirteen National League and eight tournament games. He was selected at centreforward on the Team of the Century in 1984 and the Team of the Millennium in 2000.

P.D. Mehigan (Carbery) had this to say about Mick Mackey, when he picked him on his 'The Best Men of My Time':

And the 40 yards mark on my hurling team, surely and without question, belongs to that 'Playboy of the Southern World, - Munster's pride and Limerick's glory – the one and only Mick Mackey! For a combination of skill and power, of brains and brawn, the Castleconnell man, son of the great 'Tyler' Mackey, brought joy and thrills galore to thousands.

A monument was unveiled to Mackey in his native Castleconnell in May 2013. Before that the Mackey Stand in the revamped Gaelic Grounds was named after him. Fittingly, as no player went past him easily during his hurling days, there is a roundabout carrying his name in the city.

A BANDAGE ON THE GOOD KNEE

Before the 1936 championship, Limerick did a tour of the United States, their exploits on the hurling field attracting great interest across the Atlantic. The team played three games, winning the magnificent Reeves Trophy – 'the most expensive and artistic ever presented for international Gaelic competition.' In their final game they won the Limerick Club Cup. The sports writers gave the game the usual colourful treatment:

> It is no game for a fellow with a dash of lavender in his makeup. A good hurler must be at all times ready to stop, pick his head up from the field of battle, slap it back into position and resume the fray without once taking one eye off the player he's assigned to watch and the other off the enemy's goal.

Limerick had a bye to the Munster final and they were in super form against Tipperary at Thurles on 2 August, winning easily by 8-5 to 4-6. This game was Mick Mackey's first as captain and it inspired him to a leader's role in which he scored 5-3, some of the goals being gems of the rarest kind. Mackey had injured one of his knees on the American tour and expected to be a target for some of the Tipperary players. To mislead his opponents, he put a bandage on the good knee before taking to the field!

Limerick were superb against Kilkenny in the All-Ireland final, winning by 5-6 to 1-5, and limiting their opponents to a single point in the second half. A record crowd of 51,235, even beating the record for the football final, was present for the game.

OUTSTANDING AHANE

Five of this great Limerick team, John and Mick Mackey, Timmy Ryan, Paddy Scanlan and Jackie Power, came from Ahane, one of the greatest forces in club hurling at the time. Between 1931 and 1948 the club won fifteen county Limerick senior hurling championships, and to this must be added five football championships between 1935 and 1939. The Mackey brothers figured in all of them, a grand total of twenty medals each. The club participated in many tournaments also: it has been said that they built more churches than any club in history. Critics have claimed that this involvement in tournament hurling was detrimental to their inter-county record and but for it they would have won more All-Irelands.

ALL-IRELAND AT KILLARNEY

The 1937 All-Ireland between Kilkenny and Tipperary was played at Killarney. Work had begun in February 1936 on a development of Croke Park that involved the terracing of Hill 16 and the erection of a new double-decker stand to be named in memory of Michael Cusack, but a two-month strike prevented the work being completed by the contract date of August 1937. An alternative venue had to be used for the All-Ireland.

Tipperary were surprise packets, having unexpectedly beaten Limerick in the Munster final. The winners planned their game well and closed down the Limerick machine. One of Limerick's greatest defenders, Micky Cross, played under considerable stress that day because, on the night before, a fire destroyed his stables and some of his best working horses. He retired from hurling following the final. Tipperary won by 6-3 to 4-3 and played Kilkenny in the final. It was a very disappointing game with Kilkenny beaten all over the field and Tipperary winning by 3-11 to 0-3.

The great Kilkenny star, Lory Meagher, better known as 'Over the Bar, Lory', came on as a sub and his appearance was to be the last in the black and amber, in which colours he had performed so well since 1924.

THE COONEY CASE

The so-called 'Cooney Case' stemmed from the attendance by Tipperary hurler, Jimmy Cooney, at a rugby international in Dublin on 12 February. He was seen, reported and automatically suspended for three months by Central Council under the 'Ban' rule. In due course he applied for reinstatement, and his suspension was removed on 14 May. At that time a player, living outside his county as Cooney did, had to make a declaration to play for his county every year. Ten days before he attended the rugby match, Cooney sent his declaration for 1938 to the Tipperary county board, who failed to forward it to Central Council until near Easter. The president of the GAA, P. McNamee, ruled that the declaration was invalid as it was made when Cooney was suspended. The Tipperary county board responded that it was made before he was suspended but the Central Council replied that it was on the date it was received that mattered.

Tipperary ignored the decision and decided to play Cooney against Clare in the Munster final. They won but Clare objected to the result and the objection was upheld by the Munster Council. Tipperary appealed to the Central Council but were defeated and Cooney was suspended for six months and Tipperary were suspended for playing an illegal player.

Clare played Waterford in the Munster final and were beaten. Waterford thus won their first Munster final and qualified for the All-Ireland when they defeated Galway in the semi-final. Their opponents in the final were Dublin, who had beaten Kilkenny with the soon-to-be-famous Jim Langton making his first appearance in the black and amber, in a replayed Leinster final. Dublin won by 2 points to take their sixth and last All-Ireland on a day that John Keane performed heroics in his stockinged feet in a vain effort to swing victory Waterford's way.

HURLING GREATS

Lory Meagher (Kilkenny) 1899-1973

One of the outstanding players on the Kilkenny team during the 1920s and '30s was Lorenzo Ignatius Meagher, better known as Lory, who was born in Tullaroan in 1899. The name Lorenzo had been in the family for generations. Lory's father, Henry Joseph Meagher, was believed to have been at Thurles when the Gaelic Athletic Association was founded on 1 November 1884.

In private Lory Meagher was a shy and retiring man. He spent his whole life working as a farmer and never married. He was known for many years as the most eligible bachelor in Kilkenny. He avoided the limelight and was always wary of journalists. Fame was not for him.

There is a great picture of him talking to Kilkenny goalkeeper, Jimmy Walsh, at the 1945 Leinster final against Dublin. He stands beside the goalpost, wearing a cap and a crumpled 'Columbo' overcoat with his hands in the pockets and a recently lit cigarette in his mouth. He is completely nondescript.

Meagher played his club hurling with the famous Tullaroan club in Kilkenny and enjoyed much success. He gained county titles in 1924, 1925, 1930, 1933 and 1934.

He made his county senior debut in 1924 and went on to win eight Leinster championships. Kilkenny, with Lory on board, also won the 1929 final against Dublin but both teams were disqualified for being late on to the field. Having lost two All-Irelands in 1926 and 1931, Lory won three in 1932, 1933 and 1935, before losing two more in 1936 and 1937. He also won a National League title in 1933. He won two Railway Cup medals, the first in 1927, the inaugural year of the competition, and a second in 1933.

Following his death, Lory Meagher came to be regarded as perhaps one of the greatest hurlers of all time. He was personally honoured by being posthumously named on the Hurling Team of the Century in 1984. His reputation was cemented in 2000 when he was also named on the Hurling Team of the Millennium. In 2008, the GAA further honoured Meagher by naming the Lory Meagher Cup, the hurling competition for Division 4 teams, in his honour. Meagher's house is preserved as *Bród Tullaroan* in Tullaroan, County Kilkenny and is open to the public. This is a seventeenth century, two-storey thatched farmhouse where Meagher lived with his sisters. Adjoining the house is an exhibition centre and museum dedicated to Kilkenny's many exploits in Gaelic games. Here one can find a wealth of sporting history with a unique collection of trophies and other mementos of the sport, including medals and personal awards earned by Meagher and others.

THE THUNDER AND LIGHTNING ALL-IRELAND

The 1939 All-Ireland final became known as the 'thunder and lightning final' when a thunderstorm marked the clash between Cork and Kilkenny. Earlier in the year Cork beat Limerick by 2 points in the Munster final, in what has been classed as one of the greatest games of all time. Kilkenny defeated a fancied Dublin side in a fluctuating Leinster final.

The All-Ireland was played two days after the start of the Second World War and it is certain that the interest of the 40,000 spectators were firmly focused on the events in Croke Park rather than the invasion of Poland. To add to the drama was the atrocious weather that prevailed for most of the game. After heavy rain in the morning the sun shone brightly for most of the first half, but soon after the interval a clap of thunder gave a warning of things to come, and the last twenty minutes were played in a downpour punctuated by thunder and lightning. In spite of the conditions the players served up a magnificent spectacle, with Kilkenny coming out on top by 2-7 to 3-3. Jimmy Walsh captained his second All-Ireland winning team on that day. When the team returned to an enthusiastic reception in Kilkenny on Monday night, the darkened town was lit by bonfires and Verey Lights.

HURLING GREATS

Tull Considine (Clare) 1898-1980
Tull (Turlough Owen) Considine was born in Ennis in 1898, the youngest of a family of eleven. He played hurling and football with the Dalcassions Club, winning county hurling titles in 1914, 1915, 1924, 1928 and 1929, and county football titles in 1913 and 1919. He was on the Clare senior football team beaten by Wexford in the 1917 All-Ireland. For all their matches in the championship, Clare entered the field behind a republican flag bearing the inscription, 'Up De Valera'.

He played senior hurling for Clare from 1918 to 1934 at left corner-forward, winning a Munster championship medal in 1932. He was selected for Ireland in the 1928 Tailteann Games. He was an automatic choice on the Munster Railway Cup hurling teams from 1928 to 1931, winning four interprovincial medals, and he also played interprovincial football.

After retiring from Clare senior hurling, he continued to play with the Dalcassians, and later to train them. He went on to train the St Flannan's teams of 1944-1947, which won four Harty Cups and four All-Ireland Colleges titles in a row. Famous Clare hurler, Jimmy Smyth, who was a member of these teams, described Tull Considine as being 'years ahead of his time in coaching methods.'

7

1940s & ’50s

THE LAST GAME IN THE COUNTIES’ RIVALRY

Kilkenny and Limerick met again in the 1940 final and this brought almost a decade of rival clashes to an end. Kilkenny came through Leinster without difficulty but it took Limerick two cracking games to overcome Cork in Munster. Kilkenny had a slight edge in the final for about three-quarters of the hour but the move of Mick Mackey to centrefield brought dominance to Limerick in this area. As a result Limerick got on top in the final quarter and were clear winners by 3-7 to 1-7.

One commentator in the *Kilkenny Post* had this to say about the result:

It was not the want of skill or speed that beat Kilkenny. They were out-generalled. They failed to adapt their play to the changing tactic of the Limerick men. They allowed Limerick to take the initiative and dictate the terms of play. Above all they failed to react in the proper spirit to the rough stuff when it came. They did what Limerick wanted; they tried to reply in kind.

The winning team returned to Limerick on Monday. The army placed lorries at their disposal, suitably bedecked in green and white. The team made its way to Cruise’s Hotel in one triumphant procession.

The exuberance of the occasion was due to the feeling that the unexpected had happened. Many had thought that Limerick had gone over the top as a result of their defeats in 1937, 1938 and 1939, and this made the victory all the sweeter. It may have come unexpectedly, but it was no more than a magnificent team deserved.

HURLING GREATS

Tony Reddin (Tipperary) born 1919
Tony Reddin was born in Mullagh, County Galway in 1919 and came to live in Lorrha, County Tipperary in 1947. He is regarded by many as the greatest goalkeeper of them all. He played at a time, when there was no protection from incoming forwards and a goalkeeper had to be agile and have a great sidestep if he wanted to avoid ending up in the net with the ball. Reddin had this ability as well as outstanding control of the ball. He was able to stop it in such a way that it rolled down the handle of the hurley into his hand. He was professional in his approach to the game long before it was common and he spent endless hours practising. One of the ways he practised was to puck the ball against a rough stone wall so that it returned to him at all kinds of angles. In this way his reflexes and anticipation were sharpened so that he was always alert to all kinds of shots. He was also blessed with wonderful vision.

His greatness was recognised when he was named on the Team of the Century in 1984 and on the Team of the Millennium in 2000. This was recognition for the outstanding service he gave his adopted county from 1948 to 1957, during which time he made twenty-five championship appearances, winning three All-Irelands, three Munster championships, six National League titles, and five Railway Cup medals. He also won two St Brendan Cup medals, four Ireland Team cups, one Oireachtas and eight Monaghan Cup medals out of nine appearances. A true treasure trove of greatness!

FOUR-IN-A-ROW

Four All-Irelands in a row is something special and has been achieved only once in hurling. Cork achieved the distinction between 1941 and 1944, when it was a welcome return to the top after ten years in the wilderness. In fact the county's achievement is even greater when one considers they were Munster champions six times in seven years in the period 1941 to 1947, failing only once, in 1945, to come out of Munster and failing only once in the All-Ireland, to Kilkenny in 1947, and then only by a mere point. Begrudgers are inclined to downgrade their achievements because their opponents in the four-in-a-row finals, Dublin in 1941, 1942 and 1944 and Antrim in 1943, would not be regarded as major forces in hurling today, but that is to forget that Dublin were strong at the time. Another way of looking at their achievement is how comprehensive their victories were. In the six All-Irelands they played they recorded a combined score of 23 goals and 66 points while conceding only 7 goals and 38 points to their opponents.

Nine players won all four All-Irelands on the field of play. Eight of the nine, Willie Murphy (Ballincollig), Batt Thornhill (Buttevant), Alan Lotty (Sarsfields), John Quirke (Blackpool), and Christy Ring, Jack Lynch, D.J. Buckley and Jim Young (Glen Rovers), lined out in the first fifteen. A ninth player, Paddy O'Donovan (Glen Rovers), lined out in the 1941 and 1944 finals and came on as a sub in 1942 and 1943. Glen Rovers provided the captains for the first two years in the persons of Connie Buckley and Jack Lynch. Buckley had the distinction of captaining Glen Rovers to victory in the 1941 county final, which brought to an end the club's run of eight titles in a row. St Finbarr's had the captaincy in 1943 and 1944, when Mick Kenefick and Sean Condon were captains.

TRAVEL DIFFICULTIES

Cork's four-in-a-row was achieved during the Second World War, better known as the Emergency Years. The numbers attending these games were well down because of the difficulties of getting to

Croke Park, especially for supporters as far away as Cork. While over 49,000 attended the 1940 All-Ireland, only 26,000 turned up in 1941. The contemporary newspaper account stated that the reduced numbers were due to the restricted railway service. One report stated that, 'Some enthusiasts travelled from Cork on bicycle.'

The attendance at the 1942 final was up over a thousand. One newspaper reported:

> Cork supporters were not to be dismayed by the transport difficulties and many cycling parties had been organised. One party of 50 left Cork early on Saturday and reaching Portlaoise that evening, completed the journey to Dublin yesterday.

In contrast, the third biggest crowd ever attended the 1943 final, in which Cork defeated Antrim. Nearly 49,000 spectators were present. There is no satisfactory explanation for the large increase, since the travel difficulties were still there. Perhaps more attended because Cork were going for three-in-a-row and Antrim were the first team from the north to qualify for the All-Ireland, having surprisingly defeated Kilkenny in the semi-final.

The attendance at the 1944 final was back to fewer than 27,000. It included Sir John Maffey, the British Representative and Herr H. Thomsen, Secretary, German Legation. According to the report, most of the spectators were from Cork and had arrived in the city on Friday and Saturday night.

The Munster final earlier in the year is sometimes referred to as the 'Bicycle Final'! The meeting of Cork and Limerick at Thurles had gripped the imagination of the hurling public and everyone wanted to be there. Every available means of transport was pressed into service. On the Saturday afternoon the ordinary bus and rail services were stretched to the limit. Later in the evening hordes of cyclists converged on the town and soon all the hotel and boarding accommodation was taken up. Fortunately the weather was kind and some were able to sleep in barns and outhouses. From dawn of

Sunday morning all approach roads leading to the town were black with lines of cyclists and horse-drawn vehicles of every description. Many supporters also walked the 40 miles from Limerick.

Transport lorries, which were licensed for the transportation of goods and were forbidden to carry people, were often drafted in to transport teams and spectators to games during this period. Because it was illegal to carry passengers, the lorry usually travelled to the game by back roads and parked some distance from the venue in order to avoid detection.

HURLING GREATS

Christy Ring (Cork) 1920-1979
Regarded as the greatest hurler of all time, Nicholas Christopher Michael Ring, better known as Christy, was born in Cloyne in 1920. A colossus among hurling greats, he possessed everything from talent and ferocious application to longevity and a string of records. Obsessive about the game, he worked relentlessly to sustain a formidable array of techniques, complemented by great vision and anticipation.

He started hurling in the street leagues in Cloyne, progressed to a county minor championship with St Enda's of Midleton, and won a county junior with Cloyne before finding his true home with Glen Rovers in 1941. He finished his club career with them in 1967, having won thirteen senior hurling championships. In the last year he also added a Munster Club medal.

His inter-county career began in 1938 with an All-Ireland minor medal and he progressed to senior ranks in late 1939, going on to win a National League medal in 1940, followed by three other successes in 1941, 1947 and 1953.

The first of his eight All-Irelands was won in 1941 and others followed in 1942, 1943 and 1944 to achieve a unique four-in-a-row. After winning a fifth in 1946, a three-in-a-row was won in 1952, 1953 and 1954. Unfortunately for Ring he was unable to add another All-Ireland during the last ten years of his playing career. The nearest he got to another All-Ireland was as a selector for the Cork team during their three-in-a-row success in 1966, 1967 and 1968. Ring's last visit to Croke Park was on the day of the 1978 All-Ireland. He was picked on the Team of the Century in 1984 and the Team of the Millennium in 2000.

In all Christy Ring made sixty-four championship appearances, which was a record until beaten by Brendan Cummins of Tipperary. His last championship appearance was against Waterford in the 1962 Munster championship. He was a non-playing substitute for the two games played by Cork in the 1963 championship and he was dropped from the panel in 1964, even though he was still willing to play.

Another aspect of Ring's greatness can be seen in his success in the Railway Cup competition. He played for Munster from 1941-1963, winning eighteen medals during that period. The only years he failed to win a medal were 1941, 1947, 1954, 1956 and 1962. He gave some outstanding displays during these years, scoring 4-5 of Munster's total of 7-11 in the 1959 final, which coincided with the opening of the new Hogan Stand at Croke Park.

Christy Ring started out as goalkeeper, played for some time as a back, and eventually found his true place in the forwards, where he was versatile enough to play in any position. He was the top scorer in the 1959-60 and 1960-61 National Leagues. He won the Caltex Hurler of the Year award in 1959.

Christy Ring died on 2 March 1979. An estimated 60,000 people lined the streets of Cork for his funeral. His graveside oration was delivered by Taoiseach Jack Lynch, who was a longtime hurling colleague at Glen Rovers and with Cork.

Gael Linn made a film of his hurling life in 1964. There is a life-size statue of Ring in front of the GAA pitch in Cloyne.

The county's second stadium, Páirc Úi Rinn, is named after him. There's the Christy Ring Bridge over the Lee. In 2005, the GAA inaugurated a hurling competition, the Christy Ring Cup, in his honour. In 2006 a life-size statue of him was unveiled at Cork Airport, ideally placed to welcome home locals and baffle tourists.

THE FOOT AND MOUTH SAGA, 1941

There was major disruption to the format of the 1941 hurling championship due to a serious outbreak of foot and mouth disease in many parts of Munster and South Leinster. As a result, Tipperary, who defeated Waterford in the first round of the Munster championship, weren't allowed to play Cork in the semi-final. In Leinster, Kilkenny, who had qualified for the provincial final, were similarly restricted. When the outbreak showed no signs of abating, Central Council requested Munster and Leinster Councils to make arrangements to proceed with the concluding stages of the championships. Leinster nominated Dublin to play Galway in the All-Ireland semi-final, while Munster decided that Limerick, who had already beaten Clare, would play Cork to decide who would represent it. The winners of this game would play Tipperary later on for the Munster title.

By late October travel restrictions had lifted sufficiently to enable Cork and Tipperary to meet in Limerick for the Munster title. Tipperary had prepared well while Cork, who had won the All-Ireland in the meantime, took the game casually. The result was a victory for Tipperary by 5-4 to 2-5 and bragging rights about who was the best team in Ireland!

WINNING THE THIRTEENTH BRINGS A SIGN OF RELIEF

Two teams won their thirteenth All-Ireland titles during the 1940s. Tipperary won theirs in 1945 when they defeated Kilkenny in the final.

They hadn't qualified for a final since 1937 and in the meantime Cork had streaked ahead of them with four-in-a-row. Overcoming Limerick in the Munster final gave the county hope and there was great expectation when they cleared the last hurdle against Antrim in the All-Ireland semi-final. Kilkenny came through against Galway in their semi-final. A record crowd of over 69,000 attended the final – 18,000 higher than the previous record set in 1936. Although Tipperary led by 4 goals at half-time, Kilkenny staged a great rally in the second half and it took a Tony Brennan goal near the end to ensure Tipperary's victory. The victorious captain was John Maher, who gave a superb display against the great Jim Langton, and he collected his third All-Ireland medal that day to add to those won in 1930 and 1937. There was jubilation in the county at the victory and also a sigh of relief that the elusive thirteenth title had been won.

Kilkenny won their thirteenth in 1947 when they beat Cork by 0-14 to 2-7, in what was regarded as one of the greatest finals ever. The first half was even enough with Kilkenny ahead by 0-7 to 0-5 at the interval, having played against the breeze in the first half. Things did not look so good for Cork but they came out in the second half in determined mood and were a point up with minutes to go. Kilkenny got a free and their star player, Terry Leahy, sent over the equalizer. From the puck out Cork went after the winner, but Paddy Grace cleared and Kilkenny attacked. A Cork clearance came out to the unmarked Leahy who, from about 65 yards, sent over the winning point, his 6th in a total of 14. It was Kilkenny's fourth attempt to win their thirteenth title. After the failures of 1940, 1945 and 1946 it was the sweetest of victories.

CORK *v.* TIPPERARY, 1949-1951

Between 1949 and 1954 Cork and Tipperary dominated the hurling scene, with the latter winning the All-Ireland finals of 1949, 1950 and 1951, and Cork victorious in the following three years. The contests between the sides not only decided who would win the All-Irelands but also honed the great rivalry that existed between the counties.

Tipperary's victory in 1949 is remembered for a number of highlights. Their opponents in the first round of the Munster championship were Cork and the match ended in a draw. The replay, also at Limerick, also ended in a draw on a very warm day. It was the first Munster game to be decided in extra time and the Tipperary team withdrew to the dressing room, where they were reputedly washed down with cold water. In the meantime, Cork's team's exhausted energy was further sapped by the brilliant sunshine as they stayed on the field. Tipperary's freshness told in extra time and they won by 2 points on a score line of 2-8 to 1-9.

Afterwards Tipperary followers highlighted their team's 'smartness' in outwitting Cork by leaving the field before extra time. In contrast, Cork followers complained that Cork got a second goal which wasn't recorded as the ball rebounded from a stanchion holding up the net and was cleared before the umpire could react.

Tipperary's unlikely opponents in the All-Ireland final were Laois, appearing in their first final in thirty-four years. The team was captained by Paddy Ruschitzko, of Polich descent, from the Clonad club and also included was Harry Gray, who had won an All-Ireland eleven years previously with Dublin. The game captured the public imagination and attracted over 67,000 spectators but was a poor contest that Tipperary won by 3-11 to 0-3. The victory was unique for Tony Brennan, who added a second All-Ireland at full-back to the one he had won in 1945 as a full-forward.

The Cork-Tipperary rivalry was renewed in 1950 when the sides met in Killarney in the Munster final. The official attendance was 39,000 but was estimated to have been 50,000 as the gates were broken down and the walls scaled by enthusiastic supporters clamouring to get in. Tipperary led by 1-13 to 1-6 at the interval but Cork rallied in the second half and came within a goal of the champions. There were many encroachments of spectators on to the field and the game was stopped several times until the referee, Liam O'Donoghue of Limerick, sounded the final whistle with Tipperary ahead by 2-17 to 3-11.

There were many stories from the game. Tipperary goalkeeper, Tony Reddin, was bombarded by bottles, sods and other missiles. Cork full-forward, Jack Lynch, made vain appeals to the Cork supporters to refrain. The goalposts were loosened and on one occasion a certain Cork point was made wide by pulling the posts inwards. At another stage the net was collapsed and Reddin barely escaped. In the end he made his exit from the ground in clerical garb.

The All-Ireland final against Kilkenny was an anti-climax after this drama. Kilkenny had defeated Wexford in the Leinster final and had become the first holders of the O'Keeffe Cup for Leinster hurling champions. Over 36,000 attended the game in Nowlan Park and broadcaster Micheal Ó Hehir had to finish his radio commentary of the game standing on the roof of his car, when his view of the game was obstructed by the overflow crowd.

There were great expectations for the All-Ireland but they failed to materialise and Tipperary, who hadn't been beaten by Kilkenny in a final since 1922, won by 1-9 to 1-8.

Tipperary played Cork in the 1951 Munster final and this must rank as one of the greatest games between the sides. Tipperary put in a storming finish to win by 2-11 to 2-9 at Limerick on a day when many spectators couldn't get onto the ground and had to be satisfied with a radio relay outside the gates.

Tipperary's opponents in the All-Ireland final were Wexford, who had won their first Leinster final in thirty-three years. Because of the similarity of colours the sides changed for the game, with Tipperary wearing the blue of Munster and Wexford the green of Leinster. Wexford got off to a flying start and looked as if they would swamp Tipperary but good goalkeeping by Tony Reddin and missed chances by the challengers ensured that Tipperary led by a goal at half-time and by the end of the third quarter, Wexford were a spent force. However, Tipperary's victory of 7-7 to 3-9 somewhat flattered the winners. It was their first three-in-a-row.

HURLING GREATS

John Doyle (Tipperary) 1930-2010

John Doyle, who was born in Holycross in 1930, stood out as a colossus on the hurling field during a playing period of nineteen years. A versatile back man, he played in both the halfback and the full line during his career. He is widely regarded as one of the greatest hurlers in the history of the game and is one of only a handful of players to have won All-Irelands in three decades. He won eight All-Ireland medals on the field of play and was the second hurler after Christy Ring to achieve that honour.

He first played hurling with Holycross-Ballycahill and his successes with them included three senior county finals, in 1948, 1951 and 1954. He played with the club from 1947 to 1968.

His first appearance with the county was in the minor championship of 1947 and he won his first All-Ireland medal. He came on to the senior side in the replay of the first round of the 1949 Munster championship and never failed to turn out in a championship game between then and the All-Ireland of 1967. Neither did he ever go off injured. He won eight senior All-Irelands in 1949, 1950, 1951, 1958, 1961, 1962, 1964 and 1965. National League titles were won in 1949, 1950, 1952, 1954, 1955, 1957, 1959, 1960, 1961, 1964, 1965. He won Railway Cup medals in 1952, 1953, 1955, 1960 and 1963. Oireachtas medals were won in 1949, 1960, 1961, 1963, 1964 and 1965. He was picked on the Team of the Century in 1984 and the Team of the Millennium in 2000.

Possessed of a strong physique and a long stride, Doyle was famed for his dependable close defensive play, marked by his ability to execute long clearances from very tight entanglements in his corner-back position. Individually, his mastery of the shoulder-to-shoulder charge, allied to an above average number of deliveries out of defence marked him apart. Collectively, with fellow inner-defenders, Michael Maher (Holycross-Ballycahill) and Kieran Carey (Roscrea), he completed a very formidable trio as Tipperary's last line of defence for a ten-year period from the late 1950s. Their marshalling of territory in front of goal was famously known as 'Hell's Kitchen' because of the often tempestuous nature of the exchanges which greeted the dropping ball arriving from mid-field.

CORK-TIPPERARY RIVALRY, 1952-54

Tipperary's attempt to make it four-in-a-row was thwarted by Cork in the 1952 Munster final. Tipperary led by 2 goals at the interval but Cork were a transformed team with the breeze in the second half and went into a 3-point lead, while confining Tipperary to a point in the half. They won by 1-11 to 2-6. The winners were jubilant. They had reversed the trend of the previous years and prevented their rivals from going for four-in-a-row. Spearheading a great display was Christy Ring, who was shouldered from the field with blood streaming down his face. Cork's opponents in the All-Ireland final were Dublin, who had sensationally accounted for Wexford in the Leinster final. Cork led by a goal at half-time and completely dominated the second half to win by 2-14 to 0-7.

The Cork-Tipperary rivalry was renewed in the league final in April 1953 when Cork defeated their opponents by 2-10 to 2-7, in spite of the fact that the losers had enjoyed four-fifths of the possession. Cork were on top again in the Munster final, winning by 5 points. This victory was a personal triumph for Christy Ring, who showed unlimited skill and artistry as he roved far and wide around the field. On one occasion he was found in his own goal, stopping and clearing a Paddy Kenny 21-yard free. He had the honour that day of captaining the side because the county champions, Avondhu, had no representative on the team and they invited Ring to accept the honour.

Cork faced Galway in the All-Ireland final. The Galway team was one of the best to come out of the county, almost on a par with the team that had won the Railway Cup in 1947. In fact it was backboned by some of the stalwarts of that team.

The final, played before a crowd of over 71,000, was one of the most unsporting finals ever. A game of man-marking, it was a bruising encounter and there was only a point in Cork's favour as the game entered injury time. However, during that time Tom O'Sullivan scored a goal for Cork to give them a 3-3 to 0-8 victory. Afterwards, it was accepted that Galway were the superior outfit on the day but they made some tactical errors such as leaving on their injured captain, Mick Burke, until the end.

Cork and Tipperary qualified for the fifth successive Munster final in 1954. All attendance records were broken when the sides met at Limerick on 18 July. Although Tipperary had a stiff breeze in the first half, they didn't make good use of it and trailed by 5 points at the interval. They upped their performance in the second half and were only a point behind as the game entered injury time. At this stage Christy Ring sent a speculative shot into the Tipperary goalmouth. It bounced off Tony Reddin's chest and Paddy Barry finished it to the net. Ring added a point to give Cork a sensational victory.

The All-Ireland final between Cork and Wexford created huge interest and attracted the biggest crowd ever to a final, over 84,000. Each side had a colossus – Christy Ring and Nicky Rackard – on their team. High scoring was expected but the final result was 1-9 to 1-6 in Cork's favour. Wexford led at half-time and continued to dominate in the second-half until their great full-back, Nick O'Donnell, had to go off injured. Wexford moved Bobby Rackard back to full-back but the move weakened the half-back line and with five minutes to go Johnny Clifford caught Art Foley out of position and scored the winning goal. In what was regarded as a superb final, it was a unique occasion for Christy Ring, who became the first player to win eight All-Irelands and only the third player to captain three All-Ireland winning sides.

LARGER THAN LIFE WEXFORD

The names of the players who won the first All-Ireland for Wexford in 1910 are inscribed in stone in Castlebridge cemetery. The county hasn't won many All-Irelands – five in all since then, 1955, 1956, 1960, 1968 and 1996 – and are way behind the big three, Kilkenny, Cork and Tipperary, on the hurling roll of honour, but the impact the county has made in its hurling victories is much greater that the number of honours achieved.

The huge impact made by the county is best illustrated by the drawing power of the team. In the 1955 final against Galway, 72,854 turned up, the eighth largest attendance at a final. In the league final the same year against Tipperary, the attendance of 45,902 constitutes a record. The record for a hurling All-Ireland, 84,856, was set in 1954, when Wexford went down to Cork, and the second biggest crowd on record, 83,096, attended the 1956 final when Wexford beat Cork. The fourth and fifth largest crowds were in 1960, when Wexford beat Tipperary, and 1962, when Tipperary defeated Wexford.

The Wexford team of the 1950s had something special to offer. Physically they were big men, but allied to their size was a high level of skill. They were noted sportsmen, renowned for performances that sometimes approached chivalry. Many of them revealed qualities of leadership that set them apart from the rank and file of humanity. There was a romance, an energy and an excitement about them that made them larger than life. They appeared to step out of the pages of a heroic past of myths and legends.

Wexford hurling dominated the mid-1950s. In Leinster they challenged Kilkenny for supremacy by winning their first three-in-a-row title between 1954 and 1956. They appeared in three All-Irelands during the same years, winning two in 1955 and 1956. There was a universal welcome for their victory over Galway in the 1955 final, not because of any anti-Galway feeling but rather because of a belief that after so many disappointments and near-misses, Wexford hurling deserved its day in the sun. The homecoming for the heroes lasted a week in the county.

The All-Ireland champions followed up by defeating Kilkenny in the Oireachtas final. Wexford players, nine in all, backboned Leinster in defeating Munster in the Railway Cup final on St Patrick's Day 1956 before a record crowd of 46,000 spectators. Sensationally they came back from 15 points in arrears at the interval to defeat Tipperary in the league final in May. The 1956 All-Ireland final was postponed for three weeks because of an outbreak of polio, otherwise the attendance might have beaten the 1954 record. Wexford overcame Cork in a tremendous game. At one vital stage of the game Christy Ring raced to goal for a certain score but his shot was stopped by Wexford keeper, Art Foley, and cleared up the field where is eventually arrived to Nicky Rackard, who finished it to the Cork net. Ring, who was going for his ninth medal, was so impressed at the tremendous save that he shook Foley's hand. After the game Wexford were not to be outdone in their appreciation of Ring's brilliant performance. Ring was seized by Bobbie Rackard and Nick O'Donnell and carried shoulder high from the field, a memorable event in a day of memories.

The greatness of Wexford was recognised abroad the following June when they travelled to New York to play Cork in the Polo Grounds. Over 30,000 turned up at the venue to see them register another victory, defeating Cork by 7-15 to 5-5.

THE DAY KILKENNY PARADED SIXTEEN MEN

For the parade before the 1957 All-Ireland, Kilkenny paraded sixteen players, well, fifteen players and a film star in the black and amber! The latter was John Gregson, who was being 'shot' for the film *Rooney*. In spite of the 'extra' man Kilkenny won by the minimum of margins against Waterford on a scoreline of 4-10 to 3-12. It was Fr Tommy Maher's first year as a trainer.

The game initiated a period of intense rivalry between the neighbouring counties. They hadn't met on the hurling field very much up to then but were to play four (including a replay)

All-Irelands in the course of seven years. Prior to 1957 the rivalry between the counties was predominantly at club level as clubs like Mount Sion and Bennettsbridge met in tournaments. Many Kilkenny people found work in Waterford City, in places like Clover Meats, so there was quite a lot of intermingling between the people of the two counties.

Waterford came back with a bang in 1959. Having been beaten by Tipperary 4-12 to 1-5 in the 1958 Munster final, Waterford reversed the result by 9-3 to 3-4 in the Munster semi-final. They went on to meet Kilkenny in the All-Ireland after defeating Cork in the Munster final. The 1959 final was regarded as one of the greatest finals ever, a tense and thrilling contest played at a furious pace. In the end a deflected goal by Seamus Power gave Waterford the equaliser. It was the first drawn final since 1934. The replay attracted nearly 78,000 fans. Waterford led at half-time and confined Kilkenny to 2 points, both scored by Eddie Kehir – making his first senior appearance – in the second-half. It was a powerful Waterford display and their victory by 3-12 to 1-10 was inspired by many superb displays, but particularly from their captain, Frankie Walsh, and their bustling centreforward, Tom Cheasty.

Waterford lost to Tipperary in the 1960 Munster championship and didn't return to glory again until 1963. They defeated Tipperary in the National League final and the sides met again in the Munster final, with Tipperary hoping to qualify for their third All-Ireland in a row. The All-Ireland champions appeared to be in control in the first half and led by 5 points to 3 at the interval but Waterford did enough to win by 0-11 to 0-8 in a surprisingly low-scoring game. Kilkenny were Waterford's opponents for the third time in seven years and the final score was 4-17 to 6-8, in favour of the black and amber. The combined scores created a record for a sixty-minute final. Kilkenny led by 7 points at the interval. The great Ned Power was replaced in the Waterford goal. Ollie Walsh made great saves in the end to deny a Waterford victory. Eddie Kehir scored 14 of Kilkenny's 17 points. Seamus Cleere's display as captain was to earn him the Caltex Hurler of the Year award.

8

1960s & '70s

A GREAT TIPPERARY ERA, 1958-1968

Tipperary dominated the hurling scene during the years from 1958 to 1968, contesting eight All-Irelands. They won in 1958, 1961, 1962, 1964 and 1965. In fact, the team that won the last two finals was regarded as the greatest team that ever played for the county.

The three losses came in 1960, 1967 and 1968. Wexford came out on top in 1960 and 1968. In 1960 they were very much underdogs, with the pundits rating their chances next to zero. One pundit stated that while Wexford were 'skilled, seasoned but no longer in the full flush of youth, [they] would be exposed to a merciless pounding by the searing, searching persistency of this most talented of all attacking machines.' The reality on the day was very different. Tipperary were only a shadow of what was expected of them, scored only 11 points and were outclassed by a Wexford side that scored 2-15.

Wexford's second success in 1968 was sensational. Trailing by 10 points after twenty-six minutes, they stormed back to be 8 points in front as they entered the last quarter, reminiscent of their great comeback in the 1956 league final, and while Tipperary got two late consolation goals, Wexford were deserving winners.

Tipperary's other loss was to Kilkenny in the 1967 All-Ireland, their first defeat by the black and amber in a major competition since 1922. On a blustery day Tipperary, with wind advantage, led by double scores at half-time and their lead would have been much greater but for some brilliant saves by Ollie Walsh between the posts for Kilkenny. In the second half Kilkenny got on top at centrefield where John Teehan and Paddy Moran out-hurled Mick Roche, who was captaining the first of two losing final teams, and Theo English. The supply of ball was cut off to the Tipperary forwards, who were limited to just a point, and Kilkenny should have won by more than their 4-point margin of victory. John Doyle was seeking his ninth All-Ireland medal on the day, in his nineteenth year of senior hurling for Tipperary. On a sad note Tom Walsh, the Kilkenny centreforward, had to have his eye removed as a result of an injury received in the game, and a career, that had been shaping up to an illustrious one, was abruptly halted.

THE VICTORIES

The first of Tipperary's victories was over Galway in 1958, after beating Kilkenny in the semi-final. Tipperary were hot favourites and only 47,000 attended the final, the lowest number since 1944. Although playing against the breeze in the first half, Tipperary led by 10 points in the first half, two early goals shattering Galway's chances. However, Galway changed goalkeepers and put up a better performance in the second half before going down by 4-9 to 2-5. Following this defeat Galway made their debut in the Munster championship and this arrangement stood until 1969.

Tipperary were expected to beat Dublin easily in the 1961 final because of the latter's record in the championship since 1948. They beat Wexford sensationally in the Leinster final but not many gave them a chance against Tipperary in the All-Ireland, the first hurling game to be televised. Although Tipperary led at half-time Dublin went ahead in the second-half and looked likely victors. Two events halted their progress. The first was the sending off of the inspirational Lar Foley and the second a brilliant save by Donal O'Brien in the Tipperary goal. In the end Tipperary were very lucky to win by a point.

A year later Tipperary's opponents in the final were Wexford, who unexpectedly defeated Kilkenny in the Leinster final. This game was a thrilling encounter. It was nip and tuck right through with the lead changing on numerous occasions. Tipperary's superior freshness in the closing stages ensured their 2-point victory.

Having lost sensationally to Waterford in the 1963 championship, Tipperary were back with a bang in the 1964 campaign and their progress to the final was uninterrupted and spectacular. Kilkenny were their opponents in the final and were slight favourites following impressive displays in the Leinster championship. In fact they went down to Tipperary by 5-13 to 2-8 and suffered their greatest defeat since the 1937 loss at Killarney.

Tipperary's progress to the 1965 final was equally impressive. They inflicted a crushing defeat on Cork in the Munster final and were favourites against Wexford in the All-Ireland final. The foundation of Tipperary's success were laid by 2 goals by Sean McLoughlin in the first quarter and an impregnable inner line of defence. In the end they won by 2-16 to 0-10.

In the five finals Tipperary amassed a total of 14 goals and 64 points and conceded 7 goals 46 points. Three players, Donie Nealon, Jimmy Doyle and Liam Devaney, played in all eight All-Irelands. This great period of dominance came to an end for Tipperary with the 1968 defeat. There was to be one more flash of brilliance in 1971 but after that the 'famine' arrived and the county had to wait for eighteen years for the next All-Ireland success.

CORK RETURN FROM THE WILDERNESS

Cork won the 1966 All-Ireland after being without a victory for twelve years and the win was savoured and remembered in a way greater victories weren't. They had to play four games to get out of Munster, having been lucky to survive the first round against Clare when a late shot by Justin McCarthy ended up in the Clare net for a dramatic draw. Having won the replay, Cork defeated Limerick, who had sensationally ousted Tipperary in the first round, in a low-scoring semi-final at Killarney, and went on to defeat Waterford in the Munster final. Their opponents in the All-Ireland were Kilkenny, who had beaten Cork in the league semi-final, and great numbers of Cork supporters, hungry for success, travelled to Croke Park for the final. They lifted their team with huge emotion as they emerged from the dressing room. Although Kilkenny were favourites and had the wind advantage in the first half, they led by only 2 points at the interval. On resuming, Cork soon equalised and there was no stopping them as they went on to win by 3-9 to 1-10. There was great excitement as Gerald McCarthy received the McCarthy Cup.

CORK AND KILKENNY TAKE OVER

If Tipperary dominated the 1960s, Cork and Kilkenny were the kingpins of the 1970s. The statistics for All-Ireland success are revealing. Twenty-two teams contested the eleven All-Irelands between 1969 and 1979. Kilkenny appeared on eight occasions, five times as winners in 1969, 1972, 1974, 1975 and 1979, and three times as losers in 1971, 1973 and 1976. Cork made six appearances, winning four times in 1970, 1976, 1977 and 1978, and losing twice, in 1969 and 1972. Wexford made three appearances and lost all three in 1970, 1976 and 1977. Galway also lost out in their two appearances in 1975 and 1979. Limerick were successful in 1973 and lost out in 1974. Tipperary had a lone appearance and victory in 1971.

So, Cork and Kilkenny won nine of the eleven All-Irelands played. At the same time they dominated their respective provincial championships. Kilkenny won eight times in Leinster during the period, including five-in-a-row from 1971 to 1975. Cork also won eight Munster championships in the eleven years and their successes included five-in-a-row from 1975 to 1979.

HURLING GREATS

Eddie Keher (Kilkenny) born 1941
Eddie Keher was born in Inistioge and is widely regarded as one of the greatest players in the history of the game. His club

wasn't very successful but it came from nowhere to win a county title in 1968, to which Keher contributed significantly and the victory ensured that he was captain of the Kilkenny team that won the All-Ireland in 1969.

His natural talent was early recognised when he went to St Kieran's College and he was a member of the county minor team for four years, winning four Leinster titles but no All-Ireland.

On his last year as a minor in 1959 he progressed to the senior team when he was drafted in for the replay of the senior All-Ireland. Over the next eighteen years he played fifty championship games and established himself as the most prolific scorer in the game. His tally of 36 goals and 307 points stood as the record until it was surpassed by Henry Shefflin. His tally of 2 goals 11 points in the All-Ireland final of 1972 was the record individual score for a final until surpassed by Nicky English's 2-12 in the 1989 final.

Eddie Keher's achievements include six All-Irelands and ten Leinster finals. He won National League titles in 1962, 1966 and 1976. Oireachtas medals were won in 1959, 1966, 1967 and 1969.

Keher was a regular member of the Leinster Railway Cup team, making his first appearance in 1961 and winning his first medal in 1964. Others followed in 1967, 1971, 1972, 1973, 1974, 1975 and 1977, a total of nine medals, which is a record for a Leinster player.

Keher's outstanding talent was recognised when he was selected for the Texaco Hurler of the Year award in 1972. He won five consecutive All-Star awards between 1971 and 1975. He was named for the left corner-forward position on the Hurling Team of the Century in 1984, and on the right corner-forward position on the Hurling Team of the Millennium.

Following his retirement from playing in 1977 Keher and Pat Henderson managed the Kilkenny senior team in 1979 and won an All-Ireland. Keher took over the team again in 1987 but without success.

KILKENNY STARS

The Kilkenny team included an impressive number of stars. Ollie Walsh guarded the net until 1972, when he was succeeded by Noel Skehan, who had been his understudy for three All-Ireland titles and was to go on to win six more on the field of play. There were impressive backs in Jim Treacy, Phil Larkin, Pat and Ger Henderson and Brian Cody. Frank Cummins and Liam O'Brien operated effectively around midfield and Pat Delaney and Kieran Purcell were a power up front.

In 1969 Kilkenny were lucky to get out of Leinster and came up against Cork in the All-Ireland. The latter were without Justin McCarthy, who broke his leg in a motorcycle accident on his way to training, and Con Roche. The team was switched around to cater for the absentees and this upset the forwards. In spite of this Cork led by 6 points coming up to half-time but there was a tremendous turnaround in the second half, with Kilkenny running out easy winners by 6 points, on a scoreline of 2-15 to 2-9. There were some great displays on the Kilkenny side, none more so than by Ted Carroll, who went on to win the Texaco Hurler of the Year Award.

Kilkenny lost out to Wexford in the 1970 Leinster final but defeated them well in the 1971 decider and qualified for the All-Ireland against Tipperary. The smallest crowd since 1958 turned up at Croke Park on 5 September, probably because the match was being televised in colour for the first time. It was the second eighty-minute final and it produced the second-highest score in an All-Ireland, 5-17 to 5-14. With the breeze in their favour, Tipperary led by 6 points at the interval and did enough in the second half to secure victory by 3 points. It was to be Tipperary's last All-Ireland for eighteen years. Eddie Kehir scored 2-11 of Kilkenny's total, which was regarded as a record for an All-Ireland in modern times until bettered by Nicky English, when Tipperary won the 1989 final.

Kilkenny came back from defeat to contest the 1972 All-Ireland with Cork. It was expected that the eighty-minute game would suit the younger Cork side and it looked very like that when they led by 8 points with twenty-two minutes remaining. A switch by Eddie Keher and the arrival of Martin Coogan turned the game upside down. Kilkenny scored 2-9 without reply from Cork in the remaining minutes and won by 7 points on a scoreline of 3-24 to 5-11, a stunning victory for Kilkenny and a game to be forgotten by Cork. This was the day Pat Delaney introduced the solo run style by hopping the ball off the ground with his hurley.

Kilkenny faced Limerick in the 1973 final without some of their better players, Jim Treacy, Kieran Purcell and Eddie Keher. Limerick came through the Munster final against Tipperary with a dramatic late Richie Bennis point from a seventy. A move by Eamonn Cregan to centreback to manage Pat Delaney worked well for Limerick and they went on to win by 1-21 to 1-14 and claim their first All-Ireland in thirty-three years.

The two sides met again in the 1974 final with victory on this occasion going to Kilkenny. The latter came out of Leinster following a dramatic final against Wexford, who had been reduced to fourteen men just before half-time and defeated Galway in a high-scoring game in the All-Ireland semi-final. Limerick's final against Clare in Munster was a much easier affair. Limerick had the better start in the All-Ireland but Kilkenny took over to lead by 4 points at the interval and dominate the second-half to win by 3-19 to 1-13. Pat Henderson was the outstanding man on the field while Eddie Keher contributed handsomely with a personal tally of 1-11.

Kilkenny's unlikely opponents in the 1975 final were Galway, who shocked Cork in the All-Ireland semi-final. Their victory wasn't completely without warning as they had won their first National League title earlier in the year after an interval of twenty-four years. However, they were a big disappointment and Kilkenny thoroughly deserved their 12-point victory. It was the first seventy-minute final and the first time since 1933 that Kilkenny had successfully defended their title.

Kilkenny won't want to remember the 1976 Leinster final, when they were walloped by Wexford. They were also beaten by the same opposition in 1977, albeit by a much smaller margin. This game saw the last appearance of Eddie Keher, Kieran Purcell and Pat Lalor in the Kilkenny jersey. It was third time lucky for Kilkenny when they beat Wexford in the 1978 Leinster final. They had an easy victory over Galway in the All-Ireland semi-final and met Cork, who were going for three-in-a-row, in the final. The game failed to live up to expectations. The sides were level at half-time and the game remained even until Tim Crowley was switched to mark Frank Cummins at midfield. Cork gradually went ahead and were in front by 1-15 to 2-8 in the end.

Kilkenny played Galway in the 1979 All-Ireland. Galway caused upset in the semi-final when they defeated a Cork side, which had just won five-in-a-row in Munster and were targeting their fourth-in-a-row All-Ireland. The day of the final was most unsuited to hurling, with heavy rain and high winds. Kikenny chose to start against the wind but Galway squandered many chances and were behind by 1-4 to 0-5 at the interval. Galway improved in the second-half and were in contention until Noel Skehan stopped a John Connolly penalty and Kilkenny went on to get the final scores and victory by 2-12 to 1-8. Less than 54,000 attended the game, which was the lowest since 1958. A railway strike, announced the day before the game, left thousands of supporters stranded and the bad weather didn't help either. The Kilkenny side was trained by Eddie Keher and Pat Henderson and the victory gave Kilkenny their twenty-first title.

CORK WIN FOUR INCLUDING A THREE-IN-A-ROW

Cork will be remembered for their three-in-a-row success in 1976, 1977 and 1978 but these victories were anticipated by two appearances in 1969 and 1970. Cork defeated Tipperary in three major competitions during 1969, league semi-final, Munster final and Oireachtas, and these victories, the first against the Premier County in major competition since 1957, represent the passing of the baton of supremacy in Munster to Cork. The latter failed at the final hurdle against Kilkenny but they were back again in 1970 and won an easy victory over Wexford in the All-Ireland, the first eighty-minute final that produced forty-two scores and a Cork victory of 6-21 to 5-10. Eddie O'Brien scored 3-1 for Cork but was outdone by teammate Charlie McCarthy with 1-9. Another unusual feature of the final was the inclusion of four Quigley brothers on the Wexford side. Dan played at centreback and Martin, Pat and John formed the half-forward line.

Cork's progress was interrupted by Tipperary's success in 1971 and Limerick's dominance in 1973 and 1974. Having got out of Munster in 1975 they were shocked by Galway, who had won the league, in the All-Ireland semi-final. In 1976 they came up against Wexford, who had been sharpened up by two games against Galway in the All-Ireland semi-final, in the final. Wexford had 2-2 scored before Cork registered but they gradually got into the game and with an outstanding performance from Pat Moylan at centrefield, they eventually won by 2-21 to 4-11. Captain, Ray Cummins, was the first Blackrock man to lift the cup since Eudie Coughlan in 1931.

Cork came out of Munster in 1977 following victory over Clare in the final at Thurles on a day when armed thieves got away with £24,000 from the counting room under the stand. Wexford were their opponents once again in the All-Ireland but the game lacked the excitement of the previous year. Cork were in command most of the time but had to withstand a late Wexford rally before winning by 1-17 to 3-8. Winning captain, Martin O'Doherty of Glen Rovers, had an outstanding game. It was to be Wexford's last appearance in an All-Ireland until 1996.

Cork defeated Clare in a very tight game in the 1978 Munster final, played before a crowd of over 54,000 at Thurles, the biggest crowd since 1961. Before the game began, Cork's John Horgan got stuck in traffic and persuaded the Gardaí to escort him through the huge crowd making its way to the stadium. In a very low-scoring game the much-vaunted Cork half-forward line was held by a superb Clare half-back line of Ger Loughnane, Sean Stack and Sean Hehir, and led by 0-5 to 0-3 at the interval. There were still only 2 points between the sides, 0-13 to 0-11, at the final whistle. The All-Ireland between Cork and Kilkenny was expected to be a thriller but it wasn't. The game was even in the first half and remained so until the switch of Tim Crowley from half-forward to centrefield to mark Kilkenny's Frank Cummins had an effect and Cork went on to win by 4 points. As well as captaining the side, Charlie McCarthy had the satisfaction of 7 points, including the last.

The Cork three-in-a-row team included players of outstanding ability, such as Tom Cashman and Dermot McCurtain, Ray Cummins and Jimmy Barry-Murphy, Martin O'Doherty and John Horgan, Gerald McCarthy and his namesake, Charlie McCarthy. The three-in-a-row success was a major achievement and wasn't emulated until the great Kilkenny team of recent times.

LIMERICK'S LONE VICTORY

After the glorious era of the 1940s, Limerick hurling went into decline. They promised briefly with the young 'Greyhounds' in the mid-1950s before disappearing off the hurling radar again until the early 1970s. They were a powerful force for a number of years and probably deserved more than their All-Ireland victory in 1973. Their supporters would claim that they should have been contenders in 1971. Having beaten Tipperary three times in the league, they lost to the Premier County in the Munster final at Killarney on a day that Babs Keating smashed home the twenty-one yard free with a 'dry' ball, which had been surreptitiously introduced on a wet day. In 1972 Limerick were ambushed by Clare at Ennis but they had a certain revenge on Tipperary in the 1973 final at Thurles, when a last-minute seventy by Richie Bennis gave them victory. Their unlikely opponents in the All-Ireland semi-final at Ennis were London, who had surprisingly defeated Galway in the quarter-final. In a repeat of the 1940 All-Ireland, Limerick and Kilkenny met in the All-Ireland. The latter were depleted through injury but Limerick gave an outstanding display and won by 1-21 to 1-14 to take their first title in thirty-three years.

The celebrations took their toll on Limerick's performance in 1974. They were badly beaten by Cork in the league final and the Leesiders seemed form horses for the Munster final. However, Waterford sensationally beat them in the first round of the Munster championship and Limerick had Clare as opponents in the final and managed them easily. The All-Ireland was a repeat of the previous year and while the sides were even enough in the first half, Kilkenny took over after the interval and won easily by 3-19 to 1-13.

One authority has this to say about Limerick's failure to retain the title:

There were a number of reasons why Limerick failed to retain their title in 1974. The celebrations took their toll on the players. Preparations were interrupted because Mickey Cregan was away on overseas duty with the army and the team holiday was very late in the spring of 1974. The appetite and desire to win among the players had diminished having reached the promised land. Two local factors also had an effect: the decision to throw South Liberties out of the 1974 county championship and the row between Tom Ryan and Richie Bennis in a club game.

9

1980s & '90s

GALWAY AND OFFALY TO THE FORE

The period 1980 to 1994 saw the arrival of two new counties as serious contenders for All-Ireland honours. Galway, who had a single All-Ireland to its credit in 1923, became a major hurling force during these years, playing in eight All-Ireland finals and winning three. Offaly, who hadn't succeeded in winning the Leinster senior championship before 1980, contested twelve finals in a row, winning eight, and went on to win three All-Irelands out of four appearances. Kilkenny remained a force, winning four out of six All-Ireland appearances. Cork qualified on six occasions, with three victories. Tipperary won two out of three finals. Limerick lost in 1980 and 1994, and Antrim tasted defeat on their only appearance in 1989.

HURLING GREATS

Eamonn Grimes (Limerick) born 1947
Eamonn Grimes first revealed his hurling brilliance while a student at Limerick CBS, winning three Harty Cup medals in 1964, 1965 and 1966, and adding two All-Ireland Colleges medals in 1964 and 1966.

Grimes first came to prominence on the inter-county scene as a member of the Limerick minor hurling team in 1963. In that year he won the first of two Munster minor medals – the second was in 1965 – but lost the two All-Irelands to Wexford and Dublin respectively. He had no success with Limerick at under-21 level.

He joined the Limerick senior team in 1966, playing his first game against Tipperary in the Munster championship on the day before he sat for his Leaving Certificate, and was a regular member of the side, usually playing at centrefield or wing-forward, until his retirement after the 1981 championship. During this time he won an All-Ireland medal in 1973, when he captained the team, and four Munster medals in 1973, 1974, 1980 and 1981. He also won a National League and an Oireachtas title in 1971. He won the first of two All-Star awards in 1973, when he was also named Texaco Hurler of the Year, and he won his second in 1975. Both awards were at wing-forward. He won two Railway Cup medals in 1976 and 1978.

He played his club hurling with South Liberties, where he was joined by four brothers, Lar, John, Mikey and Joe. He won the first of four championship medals in 1972, the others coming in 1976, 1978 and 1981. Grimes retired from club hurling in 1986.

THIRTY THOUSAND GREET VICTORS

When Galway arrived in triumph in Eyre Square following their victory in the 1980 All-Ireland, they were greeted by an enthusiastic and emotional crowd of 30,000 supporters, giving vent to their feelings of joy and pride after years of failures and disappointments.

Their victory didn't come completely unheralded. There were many signs of a revival of their challenge for the highest honour in hurling during the previous decade. Under-21 victories were claimed in 1972 and 1978. The seniors took their second National League title in 1975. Earlier in 1980, Castlegar became the first Galway team to win the All-Ireland Club championship. Also, Galway, representing Connacht, beat Munster in the Railway Cup final, the first team from the province to achieve this honour since 1947. Galway had also played, albeit unsuccessfully, in two All-Irelands, the second of those the previous year on a wet and miserable day at Croke Park.

Having just overcome Offaly in the semi-final, Galway's opponents in the final were Limerick, who were favourites but failed to strike form on the day and Galway won by 2-15 to 3-9. The scenes that greeted the victory were superlative and they were matched by the victory speech of the captain, Joe Connolly, and Joe McDonagh's rendering of 'The West's Awake'.

Galway reached the final again in 1981 but were beaten by Offaly. They were back in the final in 1985, only to lose to Offaly once again. They lost the final again in 1986, this time to Cork.

Their greatest period was in the following three years. In 1987 Galway defeated an inexperienced Tipperary side in the semi-final before the biggest crowd for such a contest since 1958 and qualified for the final against Kilkenny. In a tough, low-scoring encounter, they won by 1-12 to 0-9, in a game in which wing-back Gerry McInerney, who had returned from New York for the final, played a blinder.

Galway made it two-in-a-row in 1988. There was a lot of hype and expectation about this final, much of it a product of the high-profile managers, Cyril Farrell and Babs Keating. In his book, *The Right To Win*, Farrell reveals the annoyance he felt before the final: 'Everywhere you turned it was Tipperary ... Tipperary ... Tipperary ... We were the defending champions but we seemed to be no more than bit players to the great blue and gold show.' Great performances by Galway goalkeeper John Commins and full-back and captain Conor Hayes, who contained the best efforts of Nicky English, contributed to Galway's 4-point victory.

Galway failed to make it three-in-a-row in 1989 following their defeat by Tipperary in the 1989 semi-final. The game was dominated by the Tony Keady affair, who had been suspended for playing in the United States. Galway's chances were hampered during the

HURLING GREATS

John Connolly (Galway) born 1948

John Connolly was born in Connemara in 1948. While still young his family moved into Galway city and he played hurling with Castlegar. He was also adept at football and boxing. Also playing with his local club were his brothers, Padraic, Joe, Gerry, Michael, Tom and Murth. John won county senior titles with the club in 1967, 1969 and 1972, when the club added Connacht; 1973, when the Connacht title was also won; 1979, when the club won Connaght and All-Ireland titles, and 1985.

Connolly made his debut with the county at underage level but without success and this continued at minor and under-21 level. Called up to senior level Galway were in the doldrums after eleven years in the Munster championship. His first success came in 1975 when he captained Galway to their first National League success since 1951 and won a place in the All-Ireland final, after shocking Cork in the semi-final, although losing to Kilkenny in the All-Ireland.

In 1979 Galway qualified for the All-Ireland again, having shocked Cork once again in the semi-final, but they went down badly in the final against Kilkenny. However, Connolly received his second All-Star award – his first had been awarded in 1971, the inaugural year of the award.

The high point of John Connolly's hurling career was in 1980 when Galway defeated Limerick in the All-Ireland and taken their first title since 1923. They qualified for their third final in a row in 1981 before going down to Offaly, who were winning their first, in the All-Ireland. Connolly continued to play until 1984, when he retired. He won a Railway Cup medal in 1980, when Connacht defeated Munster.

second half, when two of their players, Sylvie Leenane and Hopper McGrath, were sent off and Tipperary won by 1-15 to 0-14.

Galway got to the final again in 1990 but lost to Cork. Tipperary beat them easily in the semi-final of 1991 and they lost to Kilkenny at the same stage in 1992. They did make the final once again in 1993, only to lose to Kilkenny.

TWO DOUBLES IN SIX APPEARANCES

Kilkenny qualified for the All-Ireland on six occasions during this period, winning double titles in 1982 and 1983 and 1992 and 1993. In 1982 they defeated Galway, who were going for their fourth All-Ireland appearance in a row, in the semi-final and qualified to play Cork, who had come through Munster in impressive style, in the final. However, it was Kilkenny's day when they scored an 11-point victory. Noel Skehan got the Man of the Match award for an outstanding performance, which was closely followed by Christy Heffernan, who scored 2-3.

Earlier in the year Kilkenny had won the National League and they repeated the double in 1983. Cork were their opponents once again in the All-Ireland and hoped to reverse the 1982 result but in a disappointing game Kilkenny were on top for most of the game and, although Cork rallied well in the end and reduced the deficit to 2 points, Kilkenny were deserving winners. Noel Skehan won his ninth medal on the day, six on the field of play. Frank Cummins was superb at centrefield as was Joe Hennessy at wing-back.

Kilkenny lost two finals in 1987 and 1991 before coming back to take the 1992 and 1993 finals. Cork were their opponents in 1992 and Kilkenny were outsiders, having been out of the loop for a number of years. However, they were only 2 points behind at half-time after playing against the breeze and they did enough in the second-half to win by 4 points. The introduction of Christy Heffernan and a kicked goal by John Power contributed. Liam Fennelly had the honour of receiving the new Liam McCarthy Cup for the first time as Kilkenny won their twenty-fourth All-Ireland title.

The winners made it two in a row in 1993 when they defeated Galway in the final. A key moment occurred in the second half when there was only a point between the sides. A Galway hand pass went over the sideline and from the resulting puck Kilkenny scored a goal and followed up with a point. Galway never recovered as Kilkenny won by 5 points. As well Galway were guilty of many wasted chances in the course of the game.

CENTENARY ALL-IRELAND WINNERS

Winning the All-Ireland in the centenary year of the founding of the GAA has no greater value to a title won in other years, but it does carry some extra prestige. Having lost the finals of 1982 and 1983 to Kilkenny, Cork found themselves opposed by Offaly in the centenary final, which was played at Semple Stadium in commemoration of the founding of the GAA in Thurles, instead of Croke Park. The game failed to live up to the hype as Cork proved much too good for an under-performing Offaly side and they won by 3-16 to 1-12. A feature of the game was the outstanding performance of John Crowley at centreback and of John Fenton, who captained the side, at centrefield, where he scored 7 points.

Cork were shocked by Galway in the 1985 semi-final but came back to win in 1986 against the same opposition. In fact Galway went into this final as favourites but some of their tactics, like the two-man full-forward line, just didn't work. The game remained poised until midway through the second-half when Tomás Mulcahy scored a spectacular goal, following a fifty-yard solo run, and set Cork up for victory.

'DONKEYS DON'T WIN DERBYS'

An unwise remark by Tipperary manager, Babs Keating, in which he appeared to imply that Cork's chances of winning the 1990 Munster final were as good as those of a donkey winning the Derby, turned out to be a glorious spur to Cork's motivation to beat Tipperary, who were going for an unprecedented fourth title in a row, which they duly did and went on to win the All-Ireland. Their opponents in the final were Galway, who led by 7 points ten minutes into the second half and appeared to be coasting to victory. Then, in the following nineteen minutes, Cork scored 4-3 as Galway inexplicably collapsed and the Rebels won by 5-15 to 2-21. When Tomás Mulcahy was presented with the McCarthy Cup, he became the last Cork captain to do so, as it was replaced in 1992.

HURLING GREATS

Nicky English (Tipperary) born 1962
Born in the parish of Lattin-Cullen in 1962, Nicky English was one of the outstanding forwards to play for Tipperary. He played senior hurling from 1982 until 1996, taking part in thirty-five championship games and scoring 20 goals and 117 points. He holds the modern record for the greatest number of scores in an All-Ireland final, 2-12 in 1989. In that year his greatness was honoured when he won the Texaco Hurler of the Year award, as it was in the sixth All-Star awards he received during his career.

His club, Lattin-Cullen, was a dual club and he won three divisional titles with it: intermediate football in 1989, junior hurling in 1992 and intermediate hurling in 1996. During his time at UCC he won five Fitzgibbon Cups in a row, 1981-85, scoring in all five finals.

His inter-county career commenced as a minor in 1979 and he won an All-Ireland in 1980. He joined the county under-21 side in 1981, winning an All-Ireland in that year, was on the side beaten in the centenary Munster final by Cork at Thurles, and was part of the team that came good during the end of the 1980s. He won two senior All-Irelands in 1989 and 1991, five Munster titles in 1987, 1988, 1989, 1991 and 1993, and two National League titles in 1988 and 1994. He won two Railway Cup medals in 1984 and 1985. He won an Oireachtas medal in 1990.

In 1999, English was appointed manager of the Tipperary senior team and remained in charge until defeated in the 2002 championship. The high point of his managerial period was winning the National League and All-Ireland championship in 2001.

Nicky English was one of Tipperary's greatest forwards and his talent was recognised when chosen in the left full-forward position on the Tipperary Hurling Team of the Century.

'THE FAMINE IS OVER!'

These were the dramatic words of Richard Stakelum, captain, after Tipperary won their first Munster final in sixteen years at Killarney in 1987. It introduced a period of Tipperary success.

The county lost the All-Ireland semi-final to Galway and to the same opposition in the 1988 final. They finally came good when winning the 1989 All-Ireland against unlikely opponents, Antrim, who had shocked Offaly in the semi-final. The biggest task Tipperary had in that year was to overcome Galway, which was achieved in controversial circumstances. Antrim's appearance was their first in forty-six years and they were supported by a colourful crowd of committed supporters. The game was keenly contested for the first quarter but after that Tipperary took over to win comfortably on a day that Nicky English created a new record for the highest individual score in an All-Ireland, 2-12.

The 'Donkeys don't win Derbys' remark scuppered Tipperary's chances in 1990 but they were back again in 1991, when they defeated Kilkenny in the final. This was a strange game in which Tipperary never got going and Kilkenny were unable to take advantage. Tipperary were fortunate to be level at half-time and the turning point of the game was a mis-hit Michael Cleary long-range free ten minutes in the second-half, which went all the way to the Kilkenny net. During the remaining time Tipperary were unable to pull away or Kilkenny to overcome the deficit and at the end Tipperary had a 4-point advantage.

Tipperary got out of Munster in 1993 after a stunning performance against Clare in the Munster final but went down to Galway in the All-Ireland semi-final. While everything went right for Tipperary against Clare, anything that could go wrong did so against Galway.

OFFALY JOINS THE HURLING TOP TABLE

Prior to 1980, Offaly's hurling accomplishments were limited to two All-Ireland junior hurling titles in 1923 and 1929. Kilkenny were such favourites going into that year's Leinster final that a crowd of less than 10,000 turned up to see the match. Offaly won by the minimum of margins before losing to Galway by 4-9 to 3-10 in the final. In fact, Offaly supporters were annoyed at the end of this game as it appeared that the referee called it up short when Offaly were on a roll and might have won.

Offaly went all the way in 1981, getting their revenge on Galway in the All-Ireland. This victory will always be remembered for Johnny Flaherty's goal about five minutes from time, when he hand-passed the ball to the Galway net for a point lead. Two further points by Danny Owens and Padraig Horan gave Offaly a three-point victory. Whereas the goal was a vital score on the way to victory, the 5 points scored by Pat Delaney from long-range frees in the course of the game were equally important. Padraig Horan received the McCarthy Cup and Delaney featured prominently in the aftermath of the victory with his rendering of 'The Offaly Rover'.

If Offaly won the All-Ireland with a lucky goal in 1981, they lost the Leinster final in 1982 with an unlucky one. Offaly were in front with six minutes remaining in that game. Goalkeeper, Damian Martin, was policing the ball wide when Liam Fennelly nipped in and flicked it across the square to the incoming Matt Ruth, who finished it to the net for the equaliser.

HURLING GREATS

Johnny Dooley (Offaly) born 1971

Johnny Dooley was born near Clareen in 1971 and played hurling with the Seir Kieran club. He enjoyed some success at underage level before winning four senior championships in 1988, 1995, 1996 and 1998.

His obvious talent as a hurler was recognised at county level and he played minor hurling for three years, winning Leinster and All-Ireland titles in 1987 and 1989. In the latter year he was on the under-21 side that won the Leinster title but lost to Tipperary in the All-Ireland. Dooley won two further Leinster titles at this level in 1991 and 1992 but was unfortunate to lose both All-Irelands, to Galway and Waterford respectively.

Dooley made his senior debut in the 1990-91 National League and won the title with the defeat of Wexford in the final. He lined out in the championship for the first time in 1991. There wasn't any more success until 1994, when he won Leinster and All-Ireland titles, following Offaly's dramatic win over Limerick. Another Leinster final followed in 1985 but defeat to Clare followed in the All-Ireland. There was no more success until 1998 when Offaly came through the back door, following defeat by Kilkenny in the Leinster final, got through Clare in controversial circumstances in the All-Ireland semi-final, and reversed the Leinster result by beating Kilkenny in the final. It was Dooley's second All-Ireland. There was no more success, although Offaly qualified for the All-Ireland final in 2000, only to be badly beaten by Kilkenny, and he retired prematurely in 2002 following a serious knee injury.

Johnny Dooley was a skilful and exciting hurler and his talent was recognised in three All-Star awards in 1994, 1995 and 2000.

Offaly claimed the ball was wide but the goal stood and Kilkenny got 2 further points to win by that margin. The sides met again in the 1983 final, when Kilkenny won by a wider margin.

Offaly came through Leinster in 1984 with victory over Wexford, and annihilated Galway in the All-Ireland semi-final to qualify for the centenary final. They disappointed their supporters with their performance in the final and were well-beaten by Cork.

They bounced back to win the 1985 All-Ireland. They got out of Leinster following a replay with Kilkenny in the semi-final and had no problem defeating Laois in the final. Easily beating Antrim in the All-Ireland semi-final, they met Galway in the final. Although the latter were favourites, Offaly had ten of the team that defeated them in the 1981 final, and they had also beaten them in the 1984 semi-final. The contest was close with the verdict in doubt until the end, when Offaly had 2 points to spare. One of the best performances for the victors came from their oldest players, Padraig Horan.

Offaly failed to get out of Leinster in 1986 and 1987 and went down to Galway in the 1988 semi-final. They also came through Leinster in the 1989 final but were shocked by Antrim in the All-Ireland semi-final. What surprised people was that not only did Antrim win but that they enjoyed a victory margin of 3 goals. Offaly came through Leinster again in 1990 but went down to Galway in the All-Ireland semi-final.

FIVE POINTS DOWN BECOMES SIX POINTS UP

Offaly failed to get out of Leinster in 1991, 1992 and 1993. They were back in 1994 with victories over Kilkenny and Wexford in Leinster, and over Galway in the All-Ireland semi-final. Their opponents in the final were Limerick and there was a sensational ending to this game. Limerick were 5 points in front with as many minutes remaining. Offaly were awarded a 20 metre free. Johnny Dooley noticed the Limerick goal was carelessly guarded and succeeded in scoring a goal. The ball wasn't well pucked out when Offaly were back again and substitute Pat O'Connor banged in another goal to give Offaly the lead. During the remaining few minutes a rampant Offaly sent over 5 more points, to change their deficit of 5 points into a winning margin of 6 points. It was an outstanding achievement for the Offaly men and their third All-Ireland in a fourteen-year period. It was also ironic that their manager should be former hurling great and Limerick native, Eamonn Cregan.

'WE WILL WIN THE MUNSTER CHAMPIONSHIP THIS SUMMER'

These words by Clare manager, Ger Loughnane, after losing to Kilkenny in the 1995 National League final, were received with a general level of scepticism by the general public, but they were prophetic and they prefaced what was to become arguably the most exciting four years in the history of hurling. During the four years, 1995 to 1998 inclusive, Clare won two All-Irelands, and should probably have won three, after being in the hurling wilderness since 1914. Wexford came back into the winner's enclosure for the first time since 1968 and Offaly won their fourth All-Ireland in eighteen years, having gone ninety-four years before winning their first. It was an exciting time, great to be alive, a truly revolutionary period.

A HURLING MESSIAH

Ger Loughnane has to be credited with bringing Clare to their All-Ireland success in 1995. He had to change the mindset of players, who had inherited a long list of defeats and disappointments and who believed that a Munster final would never come and that the winning of the McCarthy Cup was in the realm of fantasy.

There wasn't much to presage the events of 1995. In the previous year Clare had been humiliated in the Munster final. Although they did get to the National League final early in 1995, the game showed a big difference in class between them and their conquerors, Kilkenny.

Clare supporters hadn't much faith in their side, with little more than 14,000 spectators turning up for the semi-final against Cork at Limerick. Those of little faith lived to rue their decision to stay at home as Clare won by a point in a close game with a closer finish. The Munster final against Limerick at Thurles will be remembered more for the jubilant scenes after the game than for the quality of the hurling. Limerick went ahead early on and seemed on the way to retaining their title but Clare gradually established themselves and in the end were deserving winners by 9 points, a perfect retaliation for the defeat by the same margin the previous year. Thurles will never forget the sea of saffron and blue that invaded the pitch after the final whistle to celebrate the result.

Galway were defeated in the All-Ireland semi-final and Offaly were their opponents in the final. Clare had never won the McCarthy Cup, as it hadn't been presented until 1923. Offaly were favourites but the superb Clare backline gave their forwards no scope. The Offaly backs were equally brilliant with the result it was a low-scoring game. Offaly led by 7 points at the interval but it was Clare who were on top by a point at the final whistle. The scenes of jubilation were unprecedented as the McCarthy Cup was received by Anthony Daly in a fine victory speech.

Clare were shocked by Limerick when Ciarán Carey raced up the field to score the winning point in the Munster semi-final. They were back in 1997 to beat Tipperary twice, once in the Munster final and again in the All-Ireland.

THE CLARE SHOUT

The so-called 'Clare Shout', a particular form of greeting and celebration, came to prominence with the rise of Clare hurling in the mid-nineties. Its origin is supposed to go back to 1917, when de Valera was canvassing for the Clare by-election. He was greeted on his arrival in O'Callaghan's Mills with a distinctive shout by a Stephen Donnellan. It was revived again with Clare's success, was heard on radio and Micheal O'Muircheartaigh did a piece on it.

THE HILL OF TULLA

The Hill of Tulla symbolises the physical training which Clare put into their hurling preparation in the mid-1990s. Ger Loughnane may have worked hard on their minds but he also ensured that their physical preparation was first class. He introduced early morning training sessions, heavy sessions before games, and promoted a level of intensity in training that was new and revolutionary for amateur players. Some of the sessions culminated with a run up the hill in Tulla, at the end of which all the players wished to do was throw up. This is not to imply that the players became physical robots. The exceptional talents of many of the players blossomed and reached new levels of performance following such a high level of preparation.

LIAM GRIFFIN LIFTS WEXFORD TO THE MCCARTHY CUP

When Liam Griffin took over the Wexford team in September 1994 hurling was at a low ebb in the county. In twenty-six Leinster championships between 1969 and 1994, Wexford had come through on only three occasions. In the following spring, as a result of defeat by Meath in the National League, the new manager had to endure a string of invective and spittle in the face as he returned to the dressing room after the game. The worm began to run as Griffin's fitness program began to work. He also fostered self-motivation and self-improvement targets. In the first match in the 1996 championship old rivals Kilkenny were beaten and Wexford went on to win their first Leinster final since 1977, beating Offaly by 8 points in a magnificent performance. Galway were overcome in the All-Ireland semi-final and Limerick were defeated in the final on a day when the Wexford backs conceded only one free, a performance of rare discipline and a tribute to Griffin's coaching. In the course of his triumphant speech after lifting the McCarthy Cup, Wexford captain Martin Storey said: 'We have often been called the bridesmaids of hurling. Well, today we got married!'

HURLING GREATS

Liam Dunne (Wexford) born 1968

Liam Dunne played his club hurling with Oulart the Ballagh. After making his senior debut with the club in 1986, he won his first county title in 1994, and went on to win five more in a glorious period of club history. Leinster finals were lost in 1994 and 1995.

At county level he played minor in 1985 and 1986, winning a Leinster title in the first year. He was called up to the under-21 team in 1986 and won a Leinster title. He won a second title in 1987.

He made his senior debut in 1988 in the Oireachtas competition, later playing in the championship, and made thirty-eight appearances until he retired early in 2004. He had to wait until 1996 for his first success. Under the management of Liam Griffin, Wexford captured the Leinster and All-Ireland titles. Dunne won a second in 1997, when the Leinster title was retained. During the remainder of his career Wexford reached the semi-final through the back door in 2003 but no more titles were won and he retired early in 2004. He won a Railway Cup medal in 1993.

Following his retirement he went into management first with the county juvenile teams in 2005 and later with the minor team for two years, in 2007. He took over Oulart the Ballagh in 2009 and he won three county finals in a row, 2009-2011. He was appointed manager of the Wexford team at the end of 2011.

Liam Dunne was one of the finest players to come out of Wexford and his talent was recognised in three All-Star awards in 1990, 1993 and 1996. In 2004 he released his autobiography, *I Crossed the Line*, in which he revealed his battle with alcoholism.

For Liam Griffin the victory was the culmination of his hopes and dreams: 'Guts and determination is what won it. We paraded the full way round the pitch. We stood to attention for the President. We did everything we were supposed to do ... Mental preparation is so important. We were determined to be relaxed. We weren't going to be so tight-jawed that we couldn't perform. We were determined to enjoy the day. I described it to them as an under-15 hurling final. I told them to take that attitude. To face up to the responsibilities. To turn the ceremonies to our advantage ... We had planned for it, if a man was sent off. If we had an extra man. If they had an extra man. We wrote it and re-wrote it ... Clare were an example to us all. We can be an example to others.'

'SHEEP IN A HEAP' IN SIT DOWN PROTEST

Offaly won their fourth All-Ireland in 1998. They lost the Leinster final to Kilkenny and their manager, Babs Keating', was so disappointed with them that he referred to them as 'sheep in a heap' and resigned. It looked to be the end of Offaly's championship hopes. However, they resurrected their act with their new manager, Michael Bond, defeated Antrim in the All-Ireland quarter-final and came up against Clare in the semi-final. The first game ended in a draw and had to be replayed. The replay ended early when the referee made a time-keeping error. Offaly were making a comeback and believed they would catch Clare in the time left. They sat down on the Croke Park pitch in protest until they were promised a replay. They got it, won at Thurles, and went on to defeat Kilkenny in the All-Ireland, reversing the Leinster final verdict.

10

THE NEW MILLENNIUM

CODY AND KING HENRY REIGN, 1999-2013

In contrast to the variety and excitement of the previous four years, the traditional teams, Cork, Kilkenny and Tipperary, reasserted their ascendancy in hurling during the period from 1999 to 2013. In fact it might be truer to say that one of the traditional teams, Kilkenny, took over and were in complete control by the end of the period.

The statistics tell the story. Of the fourteen All-Irelands played during these years, Kilkenny won nine! Never before in the history of the game had a team been so dominant, since Kilkenny dominated the scene between their first All-Ireland in 1904 and 1913, during which period they won seven in ten years. As well as winning ten of the first thirteen All-Irelands in the Millennium, Kilkenny were runner-up in three more.

Some great players were involved in these tremendous victories but one stands out above them all, Henry Shefflin, better known as King Henry, who established himself as arguably the greatest hurler of all times. Equally important to this great period of success was team manager, Brian Cody, who was appointed manager in November 1998 and was in charge for the whole period, after been initially appointed for two-years.

In the early years of this period Cork vied with Kilkenny, beating them twice in 1999 and 2004, as well as winning a third title in 2005 but, having lost to Kilkenny in 2006, they went out of contention. Tipperary promised to be a challenger in 2001 and 2010, when they won two titles, but they failed to last the pace. They were runners-up to Kilkenny in 2009 and 2011. Galway found themselves in the runners-up position in 2001, 2005 and 2012. There were four other teams who appeared in the final, Offaly in 2000, Clare in 2002, Limerick in 2007 and Waterford in 2008.

HURLING GREATS

Tommy Walsh (Kilkenny) born 1983

Tommy Walsh was born in Tullaroan in 1983 and plays with his local club. While at school in St Kieran's College he won two Leinster Colleges and one All-Ireland Colleges titles. While at UCC he didn't enjoy any success on the hurling field.

With the famous Tullaroan club he enjoyed much success at underage level, winning A titles at every grade from primary school to under-21 level. Included in these successes was the 1997 Féile under-14 A division All-Ireland win. However, he still awaits his first senior county win.

At county minor level he won a Leinster medal in 2001. He was more successful at under-21 level winning two Leinster and two All-Ireland medals in 2003 and 2004.

He joined the senior panel in 2002, when he shared the county's National League, Munster and All-Ireland titles. His achievements since them have been outstanding. They include eight All-Ireland medals, six National League titles and four Walsh Cup medals.

Railway Cup medals were won in 2006, 2008 as captain, and 2009.

Tommy Walsh is the outstanding wing-back in the game at the moment and would be a major contender for the title of all-time great. His incredible ability has been recognised in nine successive All-Star awards in five different positions, an achievement never equalled, in the years 2003-2011 inclusive.

The year 2009 was probably the high point of his achievements when he was named the Texaco Hurler of the Year, the All-Stars Hurler of the Year, and the GPA Hurler of the Year.

In the same year he captained the composite rules game (shinty-hurling) team to victory over the Scots at Inverness.

Another measure of the supremacy of Kilkenny hurling during this period is the number of All-Stars awarded to the county. Of the 210 awards made over the fourteen-year period, 78 went to Kilkenny players including a record number of 9 in 2008.

There are a number of reasons why Kilkenny have monopolised the hurling championship for so long. First and foremost has to be the incredible range of talent that keeps coming through the ranks in the county. Side by side with this is the longevity of so many stars, Henry Shefflin and Tommy Walsh, for example, who continue to commit to the county and retain the hunger for competitive hurling. Such an orchestra of talent wouldn't be sufficient without an outstanding conductor, and in manager Brian Cody the county has a conductor par excellence, a man who demands the utmost commitment and the highest standards. It also appears that there are no prima donnas on the Kilkenny team, no player is allowed to get notions of his indispensability and some of the best talents have been dropped because of failure to deliver. Training sessions among the Kilkenny panel also simulate intense championship contests and players are thus well prepared for the most strenuous of inter-county encounters. There is a great desire among the panel to continue to be part of it in spite of numerous successes and this leads to a high level of competition for places with the resulting intense level of preparation.

THE KILKENNY STARS

Fifty-six players have been involved with Kilkenny in their All-Ireland achievements over the past fourteen years, either playing in the All-Ireland or coming on as a replacement in the final or, as in the case of 2001 and 2002, the semi-final. Henry Shefflin leads the way with fourteen appearances out of fourteen and he is followed by Eddie Brennan (12), Michael Kavanagh (11), Noel Hickey (11), J.J. Delaney (11), Tommy Walsh (10), James McGarry (9), Derek Lyng (9), Martin Comerford (9), Jackie Tyrell (8), Eoin Larkin (8), Peter Barry (7), D.J. Carey (7), and Richie Power (7).

11

NOTABLE MANAGERS

JIM 'TOUGH' BARRY
(1891–1968) CORK

Jim 'Tough' Barry was known as a trainer rather than a manager but he had all the functions and characteristics of the latter. His 'managerial' career lasted from 1926, when he came in as assistant trainer to Pakie Mahony on the Cork senior team, to 1966, when he helped to return Cork to All-Ireland glory after twelve years in the wilderness.

The attribution 'Tough' in his name suggests something of a big, commanding figure, but Jim was the very opposite, a tidy man. His nickname came from a boxing career in which he was a useful bantamweight, a skill he used in exhibitions for the Arms Fund after 1916. He was a very active sportsman and, as well as boxing and hurling, which he played with Blackrock, he excelled at watersports and was springboard diving champion of Ireland for four years. He was a referee and was in charge of the 1945 All-Ireland minor final.

He also possessed a beautiful tenor voice, which he put to use in the chorus of the many travelling companies which came to Cork. He also sang solo in many places including London with the Carl Rosa, Moody Manners and O'Meara opera companies. In the early days of the cinema he sang the 'Persian Love Lyrics' at the interval in the Palace Theatre, Cork.

During his period with Cork he guided the team to thirteen All-Ireland titles, four during the 1926-31 period, five between

1941 and 1946, three between 1952 and 1954, and the comeback title in 1966. He is credited with bringing a forward-thinking and holistic approach to preparing players. A tailor by profession, he visited workplaces to talk to employers on behalf of his players. He demanded proper meals for his squads after matches and was renowned for having them perfectly prepared for the biggest games. The secret of his success with so many teams was in the way he managed to gain the affection and respect of all the players under his charge. The atmosphere at his training sessions was relaxed and his contacts with players spiced with humour. His great experience and personal achievements helped to instil confidence in his players. On top of everything he had a wide knowledge of the game and his sideline moves were often sufficient to turn defeat into victory.

Jim 'Tough' Barry suffered a stroke in October 1968 and died in the South Infirmary a few days later.

PADDY LEAHY
(1891–1966) TIPPERARY

The term 'manager' as it is in use today wasn't used in Tipperary or elsewhere during Paddy Leahy's lifetime. But in the exercise of personality over a team it was he who came nearest to the modern definition of the word. First as a selector, then as chairman of the selection committee, his influence over Tipperary senior teams extended into three decades and was unprecedented.

Born in 1891, he grew up with the GAA, his father having played in one of the county's first county finals. His local townsland, Tubberadora, became nationally known by winning three All-Ireland titles in 1895, 1896 and 1898. Fierce local rivalries were harnessed in 1912 by the founding of the Boherlahan Hurling Club at a meeting attended by Paddy, and which saw his brother Johnny elected club captain.

A natural citeóg with wrists so powerful that all his life he had difficulty in finding a watch-strap to fit, he had won two junior All-Irelands before, in 1916, under the captaincy of his brother Johnny he won his first senior medal against Kilkenny when, in answer to the Kilkenny captain's post-match comment, 'We were better hurlers', the Tipperary captain replied, 'But we were better men!' He would win another in 1925, after he was prevented by the Civil War from fielding in a game that was lost to Kilkenny in 1922.

His appointment as county selector in 1949 began a trail of victory for Tipperary that was to end only with his death in 1966. It was marked by eight all-Ireland titles, nine Munster championships and eleven National Leagues. With each year his influence grew and he was widely regarded as the man who dominated not only the picking of teams but the deploying of Tipp's forces during games.

It is generally accepted among the surviving members of the teams of Tipp's glory period that his status among players was unquestioned. He never indulged in table-thumping speeches in the dressing-room but there was a personal relationship with every player and there was a moment for each when there was the hand on the shoulder and it behoved him well to take heed of the advice given.

He enjoyed a lifelong friendship with opponents of his own hurling days and with Mick Mackey and Christy Ring and other stars of other counties. But his great idols were the men he shepherded to so many victories for the Blue and Gold. In his Pantheon there was never a goalkeeper like Tony Reddan, a centre-back like Tony Wall, or a forward like Jimmy Doyle.

Perhaps nothing so underlines the difference in the role of manager today from that of Leahy's day than the fact that during his years as manger, he was also the county's representative on the Central Council of the GAA. And he was nearly 75 when he was forced by his final illness to relinquish both portfolios.

FATHER TOMMY MAHER (BORN 1923) KILKENNY

Father Tommy Maher, often referred to as the Godfather of Modern Hurling, was born in Thomastown in 1923. He went to school in St Kieran's College and later returned there as a priest and teacher. He also became heavily involved in coaching the college senior team.

But this was to happen later. While home for the summer holidays from Maynooth in 1945, he played some good hurling with his club, Castle Rovers, and was drafted into the county team for the All-Ireland against Tipperary, his first and last game in the Kilkenny jersey.

What his short spell as an All-Ireland panellist had shown him was how primitive and unco-ordinated the training was. 'Surely, he concluded,' said his biographer, Enda McEvoy, 'there had to be more to training than this delirium of effort for its own sake. Surely there had to be room for thought, for logic, for imagination, for the cultivation of science, for the identification of problems, for the improvement of weaknesses and for the coaching of skills.'

He got the opportunity to put his ideas into practice when he returned to St Kieran's as a teacher in 1955. As with the county, the game of hurling was at a low ebb in the college and he set about getting things right. Success came quickly with the All-Ireland Colleges victory in 1957, a day on which, in the words of his biographer, 'he demonstrated that the small things were the big things, that success in hurling was about mastery of the basic skills, that practising the skills was not only desirable but crucial and that practice – proper practice – could mean the difference between victory and defeat.'

Later in the same year he was drafted into the Kilkenny senior hurling team as coach. Over the next twenty-one years he would preside over an era which saw the county win fourteen Leinster finals and seven All-Ireland titles.

He soon discovered that nobody had ever put any effort into coaching the players in skills or methods or combination play. He drummed into their heads the importance of thinking about what they were doing. He emphasised the need of putting the opposing team under pressure by constantly chasing and harrying them. He had specific instructions for players in every position. Communication was vital, not only between coach and player but between the players themselves.

And there was much more that helped to transform Kilkenny hurling and make it the powerful force it was to become. Father Tommy Maher was a man before his time and for all time.

MICHAEL 'BABS' KEATING
(BORN 1944) TIPPERARY

Probably one of the most colourful managers of the modern era, Michael 'Babs' Keating had a varied and distinguished managerial career since he retired from a playing career that brought him significant success in both hurling and football. A person quick to emit a pithy comment, which landed him in trouble on occasions, he generated substantial media publicity.

His first inter-county job was in charge of Galway in 1978-79 and had mixed results. Losing badly in the National League final, Galway bounced back to defeat Cork in the All-Ireland semi-final, only to go down to Kilkenny in the final.

He was with Tipperary from 1986 to 1994 and was a major influence in bringing the county back from the hurling wilderness. He was responsible for revolutionising the role of managers, giving them a much higher profile. In fact he became the centre of media attention for the county. He also looked after teams in a holistic manner not known before. He recognised the commercial value of inter-county players and dragged the county system into the commercial age. Most notably he gave supporter clubs a status and a place in the county system, and used them to extract finance in a way not available before. He expanded the support base of teams and made hurling an attractive game to follow.

During his period with Tipperary he brought the county its first All-Ireland in eighteen years and won a second in 1991. He won five Munster finals and two league titles but the general consensus appears to be that with the talent available, the team should have won more. Particularly galling for supporters were defeats in 1990 and 1992.

After a year away from inter-county management, he returned for two years with Laois, 1995-1997 but, following some success in the National League, the county failed in the championship in both years.

After resigning from the Laois job he took on Offaly in 1997-1998 and tried to introduce a stricter training regime, which wasn't well

HURLING GREATS

Eamonn Cregan (Limerick) born 1945

Eamonn Cregan's county career with Limerick spanned the period 1964-83. He had already won a Munster minor medal with his county in 1963 before graduating to senior ranks. Noted for his skill level, ball control, and scoring ability, he had great mental strength and was an outstanding forward, winning three All-Star Awards in the full-forward line, 1971, 1972 and 1980. He was also a distinguished centre-back, as was revealed in the 1973 All-Ireland, when he was moved back to manage Kilkenny's, Pat Delaney. He was a dual player, equally adept at football, which he played at club and county level. He gave it up in 1971 to concentrate on hurling.

His achievements include one all-Ireland senior hurling medal in 1973, four Munster senior hurling medals in 1973, 1974, 1080 and 1981. He won a National League title in 1971 and an Oireachtas medal as well. While at school in Limerick CBS he won a Harty Cup medal. At the interprovincial level he won 4 Railway Cup medals with Munster in 1973, 1974, 1980 and 1981.

With his club, Claughaun, he won three county senior hurling medals in 1968, 1971 and 1986 and four county senior football medals in 1967, 1969, 1970 and 1971.

Following his retirement he went into management and managed Clare, Limerick and Offaly. His most successful stint was with Offaly, taking them to two Leinster titles in 1994 and 1995, plus an All-Ireland in the former year, when Offaly's opponents in the final were his native Limerick.

received by some of the players. Matters came to a crisis after defeat in the Leinster final by Kilkenny and some derogatory remarks by Keating of the team's performance. He resigned from the position and the team went on to take the All-Ireland under new management.

He returned to the Tipperary job once more for two years in 2005 in an attempt to revive the county's flagging fortunes. There was little success and two controversies when he dropped both Brendan Cummins and Eoin Kelly during the 2007 championship. The defeat by Wexford led to his resignation.

Whereas Babs Keating's success rate with teams may not have been the greatest, the ideas that he brought to the job of manager in the GAA context will ensure him a place in the history of hurling.

JUSTIN MCCARTHY (BORN 1945) CORK

Justin McCarthy started training Passage at the age of twenty-two in 1967 when he was injured and unable to hurl. He remembers writing notes on players, listing their good and bad points. He picked up ideas on training from listening to others, thought a lot about the game and had a passion for hurling.

He was already keen to learn more and started attending the coaching courses at Gormanstown at the end of the 1960s, initially as a student and later as a teacher. Among other things he learned the importance of communication. He put major emphasis on the fundamentals of the game, on hooking and blocking, on striking on either side, on having the player's equipment properly prepared and suitable. He was also a stickler for time and organisation around training sessions. He always expected the highest standards, which some players were unable to meet.

He broke new ground when he went to Antrim in 1970. He was still a trainer as the word 'coach' hadn't yet entered common parlance and 'manager' was still a foreign word, associated with games like soccer. He had his first major achievement when Antrim won the All-Ireland intermediate championship in 1970.

He continued the learning process, listening to team mentors in dressing rooms and picking up a lot. His next 'training' job was with Cork in 1975. He was part of the panel but when Willie John

Daly retired, he was asked to take over the training. Cork won in Munster but were beaten by Galway in the All-Ireland semi-final.

His life has been devoted to coaching and management since then. The list of teams includes Seandún, a city club he got to the Cork senior semi-final; Clare for four years at the end of the 1970s, which resulted in two league titles and two near misses for Munster finals; Cork in 1982 and in 1984, when they won the centenary final at Thurles, 1985, when they lost to Galway in All-Ireland semi; Cashel for their first county title and near miss for All-Ireland Club, bringing Dunloy to an All-Ireland Club final; Waterford from 2001-08 and three Munster titles, including their first title in thirty-nine years and a National League; Limerick for two years, and he's currently coaching Ballyroe.

EAMONN CREGAN
(BORN 1945) LIMERICK

Hurling has played a major part in Eamonn Cregan's life since he won his first medal, at under-16 level, when he was aged eleven! The game is always on his mind and he is happiest imparting his knowledge to those who are prepared to listen. After a distinguished playing career of over twenty-five years with Claughaun and Limerick which won him numerous county titles, four Munster titles, one All-Ireland and three All-Star awards, he turned his attention to coaching.

One of his earliest and most pleasant coaching memories is winning a hurling and football double with Claughaun in 1986 as player-manager. He has looked after numerous club teams since then and is currently with Mary Immaculate TC, which he brought to a Fitzgibbon Cup final in 2013 from a total college panel of fifty players.

At inter-county level he first became involved with Limerick between 1986 and 1988 but without any success. He was with Offaly from 1992 to 1996, during which time the county won two Leinster and one All-Ireland titles. Unfortunately for him the latter was at the expense of his native county. He found the Offaly players well developed in the skills of the game and concentrated on making them fitter and introducing more ground hurling.

He returned to Limerick in 1997 and stayed with them until 2002 without achieving any success. He was particularly disappointed in losing the Munster final to Tipperary in 2001 and the All-Ireland quarter-final to Wexford. In 2013 he became coach of the Limerick minor team and finds this current role the most satisfying.

As a coach he believes that the basic skills of the game should be learned at an early stage, particularly ground hurling, which some managers are inclined to pass over. It allows for fast ball into the forwards, which prevents the backs from settling and anticipating what is going to happen. Too much coaching can confuse a player and prevent him expressing himself. While high catching is important it's not the be-all and reflects on the player's opponent.

GER LOUGHNANE (BORN 1953) CLARE

Although Loughnane was noted as a great hurler in a county that was starved of success, it is for his exploits as manager of the Clare senior hurlers in the 1990s that he is best known. His managerial career began in the early 1990s. Following a short period with the under-21s, he succeeded Len Gaynor as manager of the seniors at the end of 1994.

After a winter of intense training Loughnane's side proved their worth by reaching the final of the National Hurling League. Kilkenny hammered Clare on that occasion but Loughnane stated that Clare would win the Munster final. Which they did, for the first time since 1932, and then went on to win their first All-Ireland since 1914.

Having lost in 1996 to a late Limerick point in the Munster championship, Clare were back in the winners enclosure in 1997, beating Cork, Tipperary and Kilkenny on the way to the All-Ireland final, in which they defeated Tipperary for a second time, following the introduction of the backdoor system.

Clare might have won again in 1998 but a number of things intervened. In an unruly game against Waterford in the Munster championship, Colin Lynch was sent off and received a three-month suspension. In spite of this Clare won the Munster final and met

Offaly in the All-Ireland semi-final. The game ended in a draw, the replay in controversy and Clare lost the second replay.

It marked the end of success for Loughnane's side. The manager remained in position for two more years without success. After a few years, Loughnane took over Galway for two years, 2007-2008, also without success.

Loughnane will always be remembered for having made Clare a meaningful contender for All-Ireland honours. From the time he took over as manager he set out to ensure that his players would be at a high peak of fitness when taking the field. This was achieved by an intense training regimen, much of it done in the dead of winter, which had the effect not only of making them extremely fit, but of strengthening their characters also.

Equally important was the work he did on the minds of the players, constantly haranguing them never to accept defeat, encouraging them to believe that they were as good as anybody else and inculcating in them a love of winning and the prospect of a triumphant day in Corke Park. In all of this Loughnane was driven by the memory of numerous failures during his playing years with Clare. To win as manager would be some kind of consolation.

HURLING GREATS

Henry Shefflin (Kilkenny) born 1979
Henry Shefflin was born in Waterford Regional Hospital in 1979 and arguably the greatest hurler of all time. He joined the Kilkenny senior team during the 1999 hurling championship and has been a regular member since then. He never failed to turn out for a championship game until 2013, when injury prevented him being picked for the opening game against Offaly. During that period he played sixty-two championship games, scored 27 goals and 480 points. He won twelve Leinster titles and appeared in twelve All-Irelands, winning nine on the field of play, the only

hurler ever to have done so. He also won five National League titles in 2002, 2003, 2005, 2006 and 2009.

Following his primary education in Ballyhale, he went to St Kieran's College and, after a slow start, made the senior team with whom he won Leinster and All-Ireland Colleges titles in 1996. He went from there to Waterford Institute of Technology and won back-to-back Fitzgibbon Cups with the Institute in 1999 and 2000.

With his club Ballyhale Shamrocks he won his first medal, a county minor title, in 1997. In the same year he won a county intermediate medal, following which the club was promoted senior. He won his first county senior title in 2006 and went on to win Leinster and All-Ireland titles. The club won a second county in 2007 but Shefflin played no part because of injury. He won county and Leinster titles in 2008. In 2009 there was another county and Leinster success, and a second All-Ireland in 2010.

As well as his senior achievements, Shefflin has won three Railway Cup medals, in 2002, 2003 and 2009. The latter victory was achieved over Connaght and was won in Dubai.

He is the holder of eleven All-Star awards, a record. His hurling prowess has earned him the Vodafone, Texaco and GPA Hurler of the Year awards in 2002 and 2006. In the latter year he was also presented with the RTÉ Sportsperson of the Year award. In 2009 he was chosen number one on the list of 125 greatest hurling stars. In 2012 he became the first person to win the Vodafone Hurler of the Year award for the third time. In the same year in a survey to find the Most Admired Irish Sports Personality he featured in the top ten.

Probably one of his greatest performance on the field of play was in the drawn 2012 All-Ireland final. On a day when it was expected that the younger members of the team would be setting the pace and carrying the day, it was Henry Shefflin who helped Kilkenny to draw and fight another day.